ASHE Higher Education Report: Volume 3
Kelly Ward, Lisa E. Wolf-Wendel, Series Editors

Piecing Together the Student Success Puzzle: Research, Propositions, and Recommendations

George D. Kuh
Jillian Kinzie
Jennifer A. Buckley
Brian K. Bridges
John C. Hayek

Piecing Together the Student Success Puzzle: Research, Propositions, and Recommendations
George D. Kuh, Jillian Kinzie, Jennifer A. Buckley, Brian K. Bridges, and John C. Hayek
ASHE Higher Education Report: Volume 32, Number 5
Kelly Ward, Lisa E. Wolf-Wendel, Series Editors

ISSN 1551-6970   electronic ISSN 1554-6306   ISBN 978-0-7879-97762

The **ASHE Higher Education Report** is part of the Jossey-Bass Higher and Adult Education Series and is published six times a year by Wiley Subscription Services, Inc., A Wiley Company, at Jossey-Bass, 989 Market Street, San Francisco, California 94103-1741.

For subscription information, see the Back Issue/Subscription Order Form in the back of this volume.

CALL FOR PROPOSALS: Prospective authors are strongly encouraged to contact Kelly Ward (kaward@wsu.edu) or Lisa Wolf-Wendel (lwolf@ku.edu). See "About the ASHE Higher Education Report Series" in the back of this volume.

Visit the Jossey-Bass Web site at **www.josseybass.com.**

Advisory Board

The ASHE Higher Education Report Series is sponsored by the Association for the Study of Higher Education (ASHE), which provides an editorial advisory board of ASHE members.

Contents

Executive Summary

Creating the conditions that foster student success in college has never been more important. Unfortunately, members of some of the fastest-growing groups in the United States continue to be underrepresented in postsecondary education. Participation rates by African American, Hispanic, and Native American students, first-generation students, low-income students, and students with disabilities continue to lag well behind white and Asian students.

This report examines the complicated array of social, economic, cultural, and educational factors related to student success in college. By "student success," we mean academic achievement, engagement in educationally purposeful activities, satisfaction, acquisition of desired knowledge, skills, and competencies, persistence, and attainment of educational objectives.

First, the report summarizes the major theoretical perspectives on student success in college: sociological, organizational, psychological, cultural, and economic. It then synthesizes the major research findings related to three key areas: students' background and precollege experiences, students' postsecondary activities emphasizing engagement in educationally purposeful activities, and postsecondary institutional conditions that foster student success. Our analysis leads us to seven propositions about student success; we then offer recommendations for action to address each proposition and identify areas where more research is welcome.

Propositions and Recommendations

The trajectory for academic success in college is established long before students matriculate. There is no substitute for rigorous academic preparation in elementary and secondary school. If students do not attain grade-level proficiencies—particularly in math and reading—by the eighth grade, they are much less likely to acquire the needed skills in high school, which makes early intervention even more important.

Recommendations:

- Ensure that all students have rigorous, intensive precollege academic preparation.
- Develop a comprehensive national college readiness strategy that addresses the educational needs of all students.
- Align high school curricula with college performance standards.
- Instill in K–12 educators an assets-based talent development philosophy about teaching, learning, and student success.

Family and community support are indispensable to raising a student's educational aspirations, becoming college prepared, and persisting in college. The odds of earning a baccalaureate degree increase substantially for students whose families are better informed about postsecondary educational opportunities and costs and who support and encourage their student to prepare for college. Effective school-community partnerships with well-designed college encouragement and readiness programs are also essential.

Recommendations:

- Expand the scale and scope of demonstrably effective college encouragement and transition programs.
- Ensure that students and families have accurate information about college, including real costs and availability of aid.

The right amount and kind of money matters to student success: too little can make it impossible for students to pay college bills; too much loan debt can discourage students from persisting. Affordability is a critical factor that determines whether students and their families believe college is within reach and worth making the effort to prepare for academically. For many historically underserved students, the perceived—and—in many cases—actual—cost of college is a major impediment to becoming ready for college and seeking admission.

Recommendations:

- Align financial aid and tuition policy so that financial assistance packages meet students' need.
- Create small pockets of emergency funds to meet students' financial needs in "real" time.

Most students, especially those who start college with two or more characteristics associated with premature departure, benefit from early interventions and sustained attention at various transition points in their educational journey.

In the first weeks and months of college, underprepared first-generation students and ethnic minorities at predominantly white institutions are especially prone to struggle academically and socially, particularly those from lower income levels. Special efforts are needed to support and encourage these and other at-risk students early in the college experience.

Recommendations:

- Clarify institutional values and expectations early and often to prospective and matriculating students.
- Concentrate early intervention resources on those with two or more risk factors.
- Provide multiple learning support networks, early warning systems, and safety nets.

Students who find something or someone worthwhile to connect with in the postsecondary environment are more likely to engage in educationally purposeful activities during college, persist, and achieve their educational objectives. When students belong to an affinity group, develop a meaningful relationship with one or more faculty or staff members, or take responsibility for activities that require daily decisions and tasks, they become invested in the activity and more committed to the college and their studies.

Recommendations:

- Make the classroom the locus of community.
- Structure ways for more commuter students to spend time with classmates.
- Involve every student in a meaningful way in some activity or with a positive role model in the college environment.

Institutions that focus on student success and create a student-centered culture are better positioned to help their students attain their educational objectives. Among the institutional conditions linked to persistence are supportive peers, faculty and staff members who set high expectations for student performance, and academic programs and experiences that actively engage students and foster academic and social integration such as first-year seminars, effective academic advising, peer mentoring, advising and counseling, summer bridge programs, learning communities, living-learning centers, and undergraduate research programs.

Recommendations:

- Instill in postsecondary educators an asset-based talent development philosophy about teaching, learning, and student success.
- Use effective educational practices throughout the institution.
- Use technology in educationally effective ways.
- Give institutions incentives to identify and ameliorate debilitating cultural properties.

Focus assessment and accountability efforts on what matters to student success. Institutional effectiveness and student success will not improve without valid, reliable information to guide change efforts and monitor performance.

Recommendations:

- Conduct periodic examinations of the student experience inside and outside the classroom.
- Provide incentives for postsecondary institutions to responsibly report and use information about the student experience to improve teaching, learning, and personal development.

- Provide incentives for postsecondary institutions to adopt a common reporting template for indicators of student success to make their performance transparent.
- Further develop state and institutional capacity for collecting, analyzing, and using data for accountability and improvement purposes.

Needed Research

To increase the number of students who earn a baccalaureate, we must:

- Determine the more effective approaches for encouraging different types of students to participate in and benefit from postsecondary encouragement programs.
- Identify effective ways for colleges and universities to inform high schools about their graduates' college performance and *use* the information to improve.
- Determine the most efficient way of using financial aid to encourage students' preparation for college and to make college affordable for students who need financial support to attend.
- Determine what postsecondary institutions can realistically do and at what cost to help academically underprepared students overcome the deficiencies they bring with them to college.
- Verify effective approaches that foster success of different groups of students at different types of institutions.
- Determine responsible, informative ways to accurately measure, report, and use student success indicators for purposes of accountability and improvement.

Conclusion

Who students are, what they do before starting their postsecondary education, and where and how they attend college all influence their chances for obtaining a baccalaureate degree or another postsecondary credential. Postsecondary institutions cannot change the lineage of their students. Campus cultures do not change easily or willingly. Too many long-held beliefs and standard operating practices are tightly woven into an institution's ethos and embedded in the psyche of faculty leaders and senior administrators, some of which may be counterproductive. Even so, most institutions can do far more than they do at present to implement interventions that can change the way students approach college and what they do after they arrive.

This review demonstrates that we know many of the factors that facilitate and inhibit earning a bachelor's degree. The real question is whether we have the *will* to more consistently use what we know to be promising policies and effective educational practices so as to increase the odds that more students get ready, get in, and get through.

Foreword

In this era of No Child Left Behind, higher education is being asked how it can be more accountable. How do we know that college students are learning what we hope they are learning? More important, do we know what we hope they are learning? Both of these questions are difficult to answer, but if we do not answer them, someone else will. Case in point: Secretary Spelling's final report of the Commission on the Future of Higher Education suggests the need for universal outcome measures for institutions of higher education—a scary prospect. This monograph does not propose a single measure of college students' success—nor should it—but it does offer a comprehensive examination of what colleges and universities have been doing to hold themselves accountable for student success.

Concerns about how student success is measured are not new. In 1985, Alexander Astin argued that institutions of higher education too often judge their success based on student input characteristics: those schools decreed the best are those that attract the best students. Similarly, when students were not successful, we attributed their failure to the student rather than to the institution. In place of this model, which is still too prevalent today, Astin (1985a) suggested that colleges and universities should control for the input characteristics of their students to determine the value added by the college experience. And he proposed to do so by looking at a variety of outcome measures of student success—learning, grades, retention, graduate degrees pursued, career attainment, to name a few. In this monograph, Kuh and his colleagues have done just as Astin suggested and taken it a step farther. They have compiled the most complete and up-to-date research on the factors that influence student success in college. The monograph looks at the influence of student input characteristics along with student behaviors and attributes that influence their success. Most important, this monograph examines what colleges and universities can do to influence student success. The monograph takes into account who attends college but also holds the institution and its characteristics, policies, and programs responsible for student success. Kuh also uses a broad range of definitions of student success, including students' perceptions of learning outcomes (proficiency in writing, speaking, quantitative skills), students' perceptions of personal development (interpersonal competence, humanitarianism), academic achievement (grades, graduation rates), satisfaction, graduate school attainment, and other postcollege outcomes (employment, income, civic engagement).

This monograph makes a very important contribution to the ASHE monograph series. It is comprehensive, covering a range of research on relevant input and output measures, yet accessible and easy to read. It is useful for several audiences, the primary one being those who look at higher education from the perspective of federal, state, and institutional policy. The propositions and recommendations in this book are designed to help those in positions of leadership improve access to higher education as well as to improve outcomes for those who matriculate. The book demonstrates that there are multiple measures of student success and that institutions are holding themselves accountable for achieving these outcomes.

Graduate students also have much to learn from this accessible and complete monograph, including information on the state of the literature on college student outcomes and how to use research evidence to inform policy and practice. And higher education researchers will find this monograph essential, as it establishes the baseline of what we know and how we know it about college student success. This monograph will allow creative scholars to devise new questions and research strategies to extend our knowledge on this important topic.

Lisa E. Wolf-Wendel
Series Editor

 Published online in Wiley InterScience
(www.interscience.wiley.com) • DOI: 10.1002/aehe.3205

Introduction, Context, and Overview

CREATING THE CONDITIONS THAT FOSTER STUDENT
success in college has never been more important. As many as four-fifths
of high school graduates need some form of postsecondary education
(McCabe, 2000) to be economically self-sufficient and deal effectively with the
increasingly complex social, political, and cultural issues of the twenty-first
century. Earning a baccalaureate degree is the most important rung in the
economic ladder (Bowen, 1978; Bowen and Bok, 1998; Boyer and Hechinger,
1981; Nuñez, 1998; Nuñez and Cuccaro-Alamin, 1998; Pascarella and
Terenzini, 2005; Trow, 2001), as college graduates on average earn almost a
million dollars more over the course of their working lives than those with only
a high school diploma (Pennington, 2004). Yet if current trends continue in the
production of bachelor's degrees, a fourteen million shortfall of college-educated
working adults is predicted by 2020 (Carnevale and Desrochers, 2003).

The good news is that interest in attending college is nearly universal. Nine
of ten high school completers plan to continue their education, with 71
percent aspiring to earn a bachelor's degree (Choy, 1999). And the pool of
students is wider, deeper, and more diverse than ever. Women now outnumber
men by an increasing margin, and more students from historically underrepresented groups are attending college. On some campuses such as California
State University, Los Angeles; the City University of New York, Lehman
College; New Mexico State University; University of Texas at El Paso; and
University of the Incarnate Word, students of color who were once "minority"
students are now the majority; at Occidental College and San Diego State
University, students of color now number close to half the student body.

The bad news is that enrollment and persistence rates of low-income students, African American, Latino, and Native American students, and students with disabilities lag behind white and Asian students; Latino students trail all other ethnic groups (Gonzales, 1996; Gonzalez and Szecsy, 2002; Harvey, 2001; Swail with Redd and Perna, 2003). The educational pipeline is leaking badly. In a widely cited report, the National Center for Public Policy and Higher Education (2004b) indicates that only sixty of every one hundred ninth graders graduate from high school; forty immediately enter college, twenty-seven are still enrolled their sophomore year, and only eighteen complete any type of postsecondary education within six years of graduating from high school. These figures underestimate the actual numbers of students who earn high school degrees because they do not take into account all the students who leave one school district and graduate from another or who earn a GED (Adelman, 2006a). But even if the estimates are off by as much as 10 to 15 percent, far too many students are falling short of their potential.

The quality of high school preparation is not always consistent with what colleges expect. In 2000, 48 percent and 35 percent of high school seniors scored at the basic and below basic levels, respectively, on the National Assessment of Educational Progress. Only five states—California, Indiana, Nebraska, New York, and Wyoming—have fully aligned high school academic standards with the demands of colleges and employers (Achieve, 2006). Just over half (51 percent) of high school graduates have college-level reading skills (American College Testing Program, 2006). This latter fact is most troubling, as 70 percent of students who took at least one remedial reading course in college do not obtain a degree or certificate within eight years of enrollment (Adelman, 2004).

Rising college costs are another obstacle to baccalaureate degree attainment. From 1990 to 2000, tuition jumped at private universities by 70 percent, at public universities by 84 percent, and at public two-year colleges by 62 percent (Johnstone, 2005). Those hit hardest by cost increases can least afford it. Charges at public institutions increased from 27 to 33 percent between 1986 and 1996 for families in the bottom income quartile but only from 7 to 9 percent for families in the top quartile. For each $150 increase in the net price of college attendance, the enrollment of students from the lowest income group decreases by almost 2 percent (Choy, 1999). As Levine and Nidiffer (1996, p. 159) observed, "The primary weakness of both colleges for the poor and financial aid programs is their inability to help poor kids escape from the impoverished conditions in which they grow up. . . . The vast majority of poor young people can't even imagine going to college. By the time many poor kids are sixteen or seventeen years old, either they have already dropped out of school or they lag well behind their peers educationally."

Once in college, a student's chances for graduating can vary widely. For example, about 20 percent of all four-year colleges and universities graduate fewer than one-third of their first-time, full-time, degree-seeking first-year students within six years (Carey, 2004). Data from Florida community college students as well as institutions participating in the national Achieving the Dream project suggest that about 17 percent of students who start at a two-year college either drop out or do not earn any academic credits during the first academic term (Kay McClenney, personal communication, April 20, 2006). Only about half of students who begin their postsecondary studies at a community college attain a credential within six to eight years. An additional 12 to 13 percent transfer to a four-year institution (Hoachlander, Sikora, and Horn, 2003). Only about 35 percent of first-time, full-time college students who plan to earn a bachelor's degree reach their goal in four years; 56 percent achieve it in six years (Knapp, Kelly-Reid, and Whitmore, 2006).

Three-fifths of students in public two-year colleges and one-quarter in four-year colleges and universities require at least one year of remedial coursework (Adelman, 2005; Horn and Berger, 2004; U.S. Department of Education, 2004). More than one-fourth of four-year college students who have to take three or more remedial classes leave college after the first year (Adelman, 2005; Community College Survey of Student Engagement, 2005; National Research Council, 2004). African American and Hispanic community college students who take remedial courses are far less likely to complete their degrees or transfer than their peers who do not (Bailey, Jenkins, and Leinbach, 2005)—in marked contrast to white community college students for whom remedial course enrollment does not seem to significantly decrease their likelihood of completing a credential in six years. As the number of required developmental courses increases, so do the odds that the student will drop out (Burley, Cejda, and

Butner, 2001; Community College Survey of Student Engagement, 2005). Remediation is big business, costing more than $1 billion annually (Bettinger and Long, 2005; Camera, 2003; Institute for Higher Education Policy, 1998).

Of the 45 percent of students who start college and fail to complete their degree, less than one-quarter are dismissed for poor academic performance. Most leave for other reasons. Changes in the American family structure are one such factor; more students come to campus with psychological challenges that, if unattended, can have a debilitating effect on their academic performance and social adjustment.

Consumerism colors virtually all aspects of the college experience, with many colleges and universities "marketizing" their admissions approach to recruit the right "customers"—those who are best prepared for college and can pay their way (Fallows, Bakke, Ganeshananthan, and Johnson, 2003). Some evidence suggests that both two-year and four-year institutions have de-emphasized the recruitment of underserved minorities (Breland and others, 2002); many state-supported flagship universities are admitting students mainly from high-income families (Mortenson, 2005). These trends will have deleterious consequences for American society at a time when more people than ever before are enrolling in colleges and universities and the country is becoming more racially and ethnically diverse.

Whatever the reasons many students do not achieve their postsecondary educational goals or benefit at optimal levels from the college experience, the waste of human talent and potential is unconscionable. What can colleges and universities do to uphold their share of the social contract and help more students succeed?

This report is an abridged version of work performed for the National Postsecondary Education Cooperative to synthesize the relevant literature and emerging findings related to student success, broadly defined (Kuh and others, 2006). Our purpose is to provide an informed perspective on policies, programs, and practices that can make a difference to satisfactory student performance in postsecondary education. (Appendix A explains research the methods used for this report.)

The monograph is divided into seven sections with an extensive bibliography. We take a cumulative, longitudinal view of what matters to student success, recognizing that students do not come to postsecondary education as tabula rasae. Rather, they are the products of many years of complex interactions with their family of origin and cultural, social, political, and educational environments. Thus, some students more than others are better prepared academically and have greater confidence in their ability to succeed. At the same time, what they do during college—the activities in which they engage and the company they keep—can be the margin of difference as to whether they persist and realize their educational goals.

The following questions guided our review:

- What are the major studies that represent the best work in the area?
- What are the major conclusions from these studies?
- What key questions remain unanswered?
- What are the most promising interventions before college (such as middle school, high school, bridge programs) and during college (for example, safety nets, early warning systems, intrusive advising, required courses, effective pedagogical approaches)?
- Where is more research needed and about which groups of students do we especially need to know more?

We use a "weight of the evidence" approach, emphasizing findings from high-quality inquiries and conceptual analyses, favoring national or multi-institutional studies over single-institution or state reports. Of particular interest are students who may be at risk of premature departure or underperformance such as historically underserved students (first generation, racial and ethnic minorities, low income). We are also sensitive to changing patterns of college attendance. For example, more than half of all students start college at an institution different from the one from which they will graduate. Increasing numbers of students take classes at two or more postsecondary institutions during the same academic term. Equally important, most institutions have nontrivial numbers of undergraduate students who are underperforming, many of whom are men. Identifying and intervening with these students are essential to improving achievement and persistence rates.

Definitions and Conceptual Framework

GIVEN THE STRONG DEMAND from various quarters to demonstrate evidence of student success in postsecondary education, we should not be surprised that multiple definitions of the construct exist. Among the more commonly incorporated elements are quantifiable student attainment indicators such as enrollment in postsecondary education, grades, persistence to the sophomore year, length of time to degree, and graduation (Venezia and others, 2005). Many consider degree attainment to be the definitive measure of student success. For the two-year college sector, rates of transfer to four-year institutions are considered an important indicator of student success and institutional effectiveness and will become even more important as students increasingly attend multiple institutions, as we explain later. At the same time, it is important to note that students attending two-year institutions are pursuing a range of goals (Community College Survey of Student Engagement, 2005):

- To earn an associate's degree, 57 percent;
- To transfer to a four-year school, 48 percent;
- To obtain or upgrade job-related skills, 41 percent;
- To seek self-improvement and personal enjoyment, 40 percent;
- To change careers, 30 percent; and
- To complete a certificate program, 29 percent.

Student success can also be defined using traditional measures of academic achievement such as scores on standardized college entry exams, college grades, and credit hours earned in consecutive terms, which represent progress toward the degree. Other traditional measures are graduate school admission test scores, graduate and professional school enrollment and completion rates, and performance on discipline- or field-specific examinations such as the PRAXIS in education and CPA tests in accountancy.

Some of the more difficult to measure aspects of student success are the degree to which students are satisfied with their experience and feel comfortable and affirmed in the learning environment. Astin (1993b) proposed that satisfaction should be thought of as an intermediate outcome of college. Taken together, students' impressions of institutional quality, their willingness to attend the institution again, and overall satisfaction are precursors of educational attainment and other dimensions of student success (Hossler, Schmit, and Vesper, 1999; Strauss and Volkwein, 2002).

Student success is also linked with a plethora of desired student and personal development outcomes that confer benefits on individuals and society. They include a range of learning and personal development domains such as cognitive complexity, knowledge acquisition and use, humanitarianism, interpersonal competence, and practical competence (Kuh, 1993); becoming proficient in writing, speaking, critical thinking, scientific literacy, and quantitative skills; and employment, postcollege income, civic engagement, and job and life satisfaction. Although cognitive development and direct measures of student learning are of great value, relatively few studies provide conclusive evidence about the performance of large numbers of students at individual institutions (Association of American Colleges and Universities, 2005; National Center for Public Policy and Higher Education, 2004b; Pascarella and Terenzini, 2005). We do not address these important outcomes in this volume, but Pascarella and Terenzini (2005) provide an excellent summary (see also Kuh, Douglas, Lund, and Ramin-Gyurnek, 1994; Kuh and others, 2006).

All these measures of student success have been explored to varying degrees in the literature, and observers generally agree as to their importance. In recent years, a handful of additional elements of student success have emerged representing new dimensions, variations on common indicators, and harder-to-measure ineffable qualities. Examples of such indicators are an appreciation for human differences, commitment to democratic values, a capacity to work effectively with people from different backgrounds to solve problems, information literacy, and a well-developed sense of identity (Association of American Colleges and Universities, 2002; Baxter Magolda, 2001, 2004).

Novel definitions are born out of ingenuity and necessity and may require multidimensional measures, given the increased complexity of the postmodern world and the need for institutions to be more inclusive of a much more diverse student population. For example, although the educational progress of women and minority groups has long been an important policy concern, trend analyses by gender or race typically mask important in-group differences with regard to *access* and *participation* (as distinguished from enrollment) rates in postsecondary education. That is, enrollment rates are often calculated as the percentage of high school graduates who are currently in postsecondary education. To more accurately reflect the educational progress of the nation, the proportion of a total age cohort enrolled in postsecondary education or that has completed at least two years of postsecondary education should be calculated. Such analyses better represent racial and ethnic differences in educational progress because the lower high school completion rates of minorities are taken into account (U.S. Department of Education, 1997, 2003b).

Definitions of student success must be sensitive to economic realities and workforce development needs. A high school education is no longer sufficient to succeed in college and the workforce in the twenty-first century (American Diploma Project, 2004). Student success indicators also must be broadened to take into account different types of students such as adult learners and transfer students as well as acknowledge different participation patterns represented by course retention rates and posttransfer performance. Research on student persistence is another area where new concepts have emerged. Studies of first-generation students, adult learners, commuters, and other underrepresented populations show that external factors such as parental encouragement, student expectations, peer support, and finances are important to persistence (Braxton, Hirschy, and McClendon, 2004; Cabrera, Casteneda, Nora, and Hengstler, 1992; Pascarella, Pierson, Wolniak, and Terenzini, 2004; Pike and Kuh, 2005a; Swail, Cabrera, Lee, and Williams, 2005; Terenzini and others, 1996). Adult learners pursue postsecondary education for a range of reasons, including wanting to be better educated, informed citizens (49 percent), enhancing personal happiness and satisfaction (47 percent), obtaining a higher degree (43 percent), making more money (33 percent), and meeting job requirements (33 percent) (Bradburn and Hurst, 2001). For this reason, academic and social self-confidence and self-esteem are other important student outcomes that are receiving more attention. In fact, Rendon (1995) found that the most important indicators of Latino student success include believing in one's ability to perform in college, believing in one's capacity as a learner, being excited about learning, and feeling cared about as a student and a person.

Student engagement is another indicator of student success that has received considerable attention in recent years (Kuh, 2001, 2003; Pascarella and Terenzini, 2005). As mentioned earlier, a substantial body of research indicates that once students start college, a key factor to whether they will survive and thrive in college is the extent to which students take part in educationally effective activities.

A broad, holistic definition of student success must include all of these indicators and speak to three questions:

1. What do we want and need of students before and after they enroll in postsecondary education?
2. What happens to students during their postsecondary studies?
3. What are the implications of these definitions for informing policy and practice and improving student and institutional performance?

For purposes of this report, student success is defined as academic achievement; engagement in educationally purposeful activities; satisfaction; acquisition of desired knowledge, skills, and competencies; persistence; and attainment of educational objectives.

Figure 1 is the guiding framework for our analysis. Instead of the familiar "pipeline" analogy depicted by a direct route to educational attainment, a more accurate representation is a wide path with twists, turns, detours, roundabouts, and occasional dead ends that many students encounter.

The first section of the path represents students' precollege experiences. We summarize the effects of family background, their precollege academic preparation, enrollment choices, and financial aid and assistance policies on various dimensions of student success. In Figure 1, mediating conditions are represented as transitions that students must successfully navigate to continue their

FIGURE 1
What Matters to Student Success

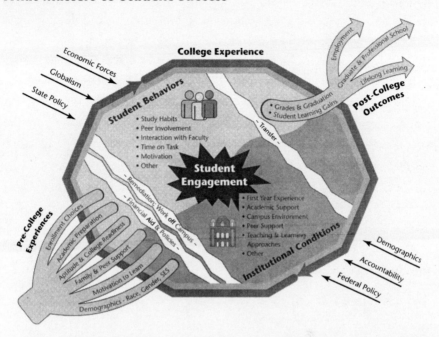

education. They include remediation courses that do not count toward graduation but are necessary to acquire college-level academic skills, financial aid policies that facilitate or hinder their continued enrollment, and the need to work many hours off campus, which can prohibit students from fully engaging in the college experience. If students do not successfully navigate these screens, they may be temporarily or permanently separated from the college experience.

The next part of the path—the college experience itself—includes two dimensions: *student behaviors* and *institutional conditions.* Student behaviors include such aspects as the time and effort students put into their studies, interaction with faculty, and peer involvement. Institutional conditions include resources, educational policies, programs and practices, and structural features.

At the intersection of student behaviors and institutional conditions is student engagement, which represents aspects of student behavior and institutional performance that colleges and universities can do something about, at least on the margins. High levels of purposeful student-faculty contact and active and collaborative learning supported by institutional environments perceived by students as inclusive and affirming are related to student satisfaction, persistence, educational attainment, and learning and development across a variety of dimensions (Astin, 1984, 1991; Chickering and Gamson, 1987; Chickering and Reisser, 1993; Kuh and others, 1991; Pascarella, 2001; Pascarella and Terenzini, 1991, 2005; Pike, 1993; Sorcinelli, 1991).

All these factors are inextricably intertwined and affect what students do during college and how they grow, change, and benefit in other ways from the experience. The next section briefly reviews the major theoretical perspectives that help explain student success.

Major Theoretical Perspectives on Student Success in College

A HANDFUL OF SOUND, INSTRUCTIVE PERSPECTIVES are available to guide research and practice related to fostering student success in college. As we shall see, no single view is comprehensive enough to account for the complicated set of factors that interact to influence student and institutional performance, what Braxton (2000, p. 1) calls "the departure puzzle."

The most often cited theories define student success in college as persistence and educational attainment, or achieving the desired degree or educational credential. They emphasize to varying degrees the importance of academic preparation and the quality of student experiences during college. We adapted Tinto's theory (1986) and Braxton's framework (2003) of college student departure to summarize five theoretical perspectives: sociological, organizational, psychological, cultural, and economic.

Sociological Perspectives

Tinto's interactionalist theory (1975, 1987, 1993) enjoys "near paradigmatic status" (Braxton, Sullivan, and Johnson, 1997; Pascarella and Terenzini, 2005). Grounded in Van Gennep's anthropological model of cultural rites of passage (1960), Tinto postulates that students first must separate from the group with which they were formerly associated such as family members and high school peers, undergo a period of transition "during which the person begins to interact in new ways with the members of the new group into which membership is sought" (Tinto, 1993, p. 93), and incorporate or adopt the normative values and behaviors of the new group (or college). Students who leave college are those who are unable to effectively distance themselves from their family or community of origin and adopt the values and the behavioral patterns that typify the environment of the institution they are attending.

Academic and social integration are presented as complementary but independent processes by which students adjust to college life. Academic integration represents both satisfactory compliance with explicit norms such as earning passing grades and the normative academic values of the institution such as an engineering school that values the physical sciences over the arts. Social integration represents the extent to which a student finds the institution's social environment to be congenial with his or her preferences, which are shaped by the student's background, values, and aspirations. Social integration is often measured as a composite of interactions with peers and interactions between faculty and students, while academic integration reflects satisfaction with academic progress and choice of major (Kuh, Douglas, Lund, and Ramin-Gyurnek, 1994). Thus student persistence is a function of dynamic relationships between the individual and other actors in the college and the home community. Increased levels of academic and social integration are presumed to lead to greater commitment to the institution and to the goal of graduation (Bean, 1983). These commitments in turn increase the likelihood a student will persist and graduate.

Despite its popularity, Tinto's theory has only modest empirical support. For example, only eight of the eleven multi-institutional studies that attempted to link academic integration and persistence provided support for the relationship. Single-institution studies examining the relationship between academic integration and persistence are less clear. Nineteen of forty studies (Braxton, Sullivan, and Johnson, 1997) examined did not indicate a link between persistence and academic integration. Support for social integration as a predictor of persistence is more robust than for academic integration, suggesting that increasing social integration leads to greater institutional commitment and thus greater likelihood of persistence to graduation.

Although some disagree about how best to operationalize various components of the Tinto model, most agree that for students to succeed in college, they must learn to negotiate foreign environments and interact effectively with strangers (Kuh and Love, 2000). Thus, interpersonal relationships both on and off campus may mediate student success in college. This view is consistent with a social networks perspective that college students' relationships with faculty and staff and peers as well as family, friends, and mentors contribute to student satisfaction, persistence, and what students gain from college (Astin, 1977, 1993b; Kuh, Kinzie, Schuh, Whitt, and Associates, 2005; Kuh and others, 1991; Pascarella and Terenzini, 1991, 2005; Tinto, 1975, 1987, 1993).

Social networks are "structures of relationships linking social actors" (Marsden, 2004, p. 2727) and help explain why social integration is more difficult for certain groups of students, while the family influence is all the more influential (Chamberlain, 2005). For example, Berger and Milem (1999) found that the students most likely to persist are those whose values, norms, and behavior are already congruent with dominant patterns on campus. They, along with Attinasi (1989), emphasized the importance of making connections early with peers and faculty members. Kenny and Stryker (1996) found that social adjustment to college for racially and ethnically diverse students was primarily a function of their family support networks; for white students, however, social adjustment was more strongly tied to college friendship networks.

Organizational Perspectives

Organizational perspectives emphasize the institutional structures and processes thought to affect student performance. Among the more important features are institutional size, selectivity, resources, and faculty-student ratios. For example, negative perceptions of the campus environment are associated with a variety of general institutional characteristics, including size, control, mission, and location (urban, suburban, rural) (Pike and Kuh, 2005b). Bean's student attrition model (1983) posits that beliefs shape attitudes, attitudes shape behaviors, and behaviors signal intents. A student's beliefs are affected by experiences with the institution, which then evolve into attitudes about the institution, which ultimately determine a student's sense of belonging or "fit" with the institution. Thus, students' perceptions of the fairness of institutional policies and the responsiveness of faculty and staff presumably affect decisions to persist or leave the institution. Similarly, the leadership and decision-making approaches favored by senior administrators presumably affect student satisfaction and adjustment (Berger and Braxton, 1998). The links between these features of institutional functioning and student behavior, however, are not well explicated and, in Braxton's judgment (2003), lack explanatory power.

Psychological Perspectives

Bean and Eaton (2000) used attitude-behavior theory to propose that personality traits such as self-efficacy help a student persevere when faced with academic and social challenges; those with a strong, better-developed self-concept are more confident about their ability to succeed, while those who are less confident are more likely to founder and give up when encountering difficult circumstances. Similarly, students guided by an internal locus of control believe they can work their way through situations, while those who are externally controlled may conclude that fate has determined their course, especially when facing trying times; as a consequence, they may give up and leave college prematurely. Expectancy theory, self-efficacy theory, and motivational theory suggest that students are predisposed to seek out certain kinds of activities during college (Kuh, 1999; Olsen and others, 1998), such as how to spend time, which, in turn, affects their performance inside and outside the classroom (Bandura, 1982; Dweck and Leggett, 1988). Psychological contract theory (Rousseau, 1995) presumes that students arrive with beliefs about the appropriate nature of relationships with peers, faculty, and staff and how one is to respond to various groups and the institution. When the student perceives the contract is breached, the student may lose trust in the institution, as represented by peers or faculty. Thus, what students generally expect to have happen when they start college shapes their behavior, which, in turn, affects their academic performance and social adjustment to college life (Howard, 2005; Kuh, 1999).

Dweck's work on self-theories about intelligence (2000) holds that students hold either an entity view or an incremental view of their ability. In the former, intelligence is essentially fixed; in the latter, intelligence is something that can be expanded through continued learning and experience. Dweck discovered that students' views of their abilities can be altered by structuring early learning experiences in a new subject by starting with what students are good at. "Those who are led to believe their intelligence is a malleable quality begin to take on challenging learning tasks and begin to take advantage of the skill-improvement opportunities that come their way" (p. 26). This work has powerful implications for many historically underserved students who have doubts about their abilities to do college-level work and persist to graduation (Kuh, Kinzie, Schuh, Whitt, and Associates, 2005) and for faculty members who need to understand the consequences of prematurely judging their students' talents and abilities.

Cultural Perspectives

Cultural perspectives suggest that many historically underrepresented students encounter challenges when they get to college that make it difficult for them to take advantage of their school's resources for learning and personal development. Student perceptions of the institutional environment and dominant norms and values influence how students think and spend their time. Taken together, these properties influence student satisfaction and the extent to which they engage in educationally purposeful activities (Astin, 1977, 1993b; Kuh and others, 1991; Kuh, Kinzie, Schuh, Whitt, and Associates, 2005; Kuh and Whitt, 1988; Pascarella and Terenzini, 1991, 1995). From this perspective, student-institution fit models of adjustment such as Tinto's may feature culturally biased assumptions about what is necessary to survive and thrive in college (Attinasi, 1989, 1992; Gonzalez, 2000–01; Kuh and Love, 2000; Rendon, Jalomo, and Nora, 2000; Tierney, 1992, 1993). The point of contention is whether students need to or should be expected to conform to prevailing institutional norms and mores if they conflict with those of their family of origin (Tierney, 1992). Jalomo (1995) found, for example, that Latino community college students were able to successfully operate in the multiple contexts of home and school but that the transitions were challenging. Successfully navigating dual environments of home and college,

Rendon, Jalomo, and Nora (2000) argue, is the responsibility of, and demands effort by, both the individual and the institution; students should not be left to manage and resolve these differences on their own, especially when the college environment values conventions and traditions that students perceive to be alien or antithetical to their own. It is especially challenging for first-generation students from minority racial and ethnic backgrounds who stand on the margins of two cultures: their friends and family at home and the college community (London, 1989). Many of these students experience going to college as severing important relationships at the same time that they are trying to resolve the conflicts generated by the pressures to succeed educationally and family perceptions that they are rejecting traditional family norms and values by being in college (Gonzalez, 2000–01; Nuñez and Cuccaro-Alamin, 1998; Ortiz, 2004; Torres, 2003). These tensions (often stronger for Latinas, traditionally expected to remain at home) stem not just from simply leaving home, an experience that may not seem as significant to them as actually being away from home.

A related concept is *habitus,* or a system of enduring dispositions that incorporates previous experiences that can impose unconscious limits on an individual's educational and career aspirations (Bourdieu and Passeron, 1977). Because habitus shapes individual actions such as choosing a major field or identifying opportunities in the college environment such as doing research with a faculty member or studying abroad, it can be a heuristic for understanding complex and deep-rooted patterns that make it difficult for historically underserved students to use the learning resources available on college campuses. Although habitus can perpetuate self-conceptions of low status and may predispose students to use less productive educational strategies, it also has a dynamic component that allows the possibility that students can adopt new approaches to managing academic and social challenges. Developing new ways of responding can be induced by different circumstances such as encountering new situations or interacting with people from very different backgrounds, all of which occur with regularity in the college environment (Harker, 1984; Lamont and Lareau, 1988). Another desirable outcome of such experiences is developing higher aspirations for academic achievement and personal development.

Economic Perspectives

One more way of understanding the factors that influence student departure is to consider the costs and benefits of staying in college and participating in various activities. If a student perceives that the cost of staying in school or becoming involved in a certain activity—such as orientation, a first-year seminar, internship, or study abroad—outweighs the return on investment, he or she may forgo the opportunity and leave college prematurely (Braxton, 2003). Costs include tuition and fees as well as lost income; benefits represent future earnings and other less tangible outcomes such as obtaining additional knowledge and skills and enjoying a higher overall quality of life (Goldin, Katz, and Kuziemko, 2006). Consistent with a human capital model (Becker, 1964), colleges can help create additional economic incentives for students to persist by making them aware of the benefits they will realize in their knowledge, critical thinking abilities, and sensibilities and dispositions that support lifelong learning (discussed later) and how these benefits increase their chances to obtain a desirable job and live a satisfying life after college.

Summary

No one theoretical perspective can adequately account for all the factors that influence student success in college. After evaluating Tinto's model of student integration (1987) and Bean's model of student attrition (1983), Cabrera, Casteneda, Nora, and Hengstler (1992) determined that, based on the number of hypotheses validated, the student integration model was more robust than the student attrition model; 70 percent of the hypotheses were supported compared with only 40 percent for the student attrition model. But the student attrition model accounted for more variance in student intent to persist (60 percent versus 36 percent) and persistence (44 percent versus 38 percent), a finding these researchers attributed to parental and peer encouragement and support and to finances. They concluded that these two dominant perspectives are complementary, not mutually exclusive.

Taken together, the different theoretical perspectives on student success and departure account for many of the key factors that shape what students are prepared to do when they get to college and influence the meanings they make of their experiences. In their review of the theoretical perspectives on educational attainment and persistence, Pascarella and Terenzini (2005, p. 425) concluded that the theories emphasize "a series of academic and social encounters, experiences, and forces ... [that] can be portrayed generally as the notions of academic or social engagement or the extent to which students become involved ... (Astin, 1985[b]) or integrated (Tinto, 1975, 1987, 1993) [in] their institution's academic and social systems." This observation is important, as we shall see later.

The Foundation for Student Success: Student Background Characteristics, Precollege Experiences, and Enrollment Patterns

W HO STUDENTS ARE AND WHAT THEY DO before starting their postsecondary education make a difference in their chances for obtaining a baccalaureate degree or another postsecondary credential. This section distills the major findings from the literature about student background characteristics and precollege experiences related to student success in various postsecondary settings, including two-year and four-year colleges and special-mission institutions. The literature is all but silent on the student experience at private for-profit institutions, so this growing segment of postsecondary education is not addressed. As introduced in Figure 1 and shown in Figure 2, the variables of interest include gender, race and ethnicity, academic preparation, educational aspirations, socioeconomic status (SES), motivation to learn, and the college choice process, which are mediated by college costs and availability of financial aid. We also summarize the relative literature on expectations entering students have for their experience, because it appears to influence the kinds of activities they engage in after they enroll.

Student Demographics

It is sometimes said when predicting future events that demographics is destiny. This observation holds when it comes to accounting for what matters to student success in college.

FIGURE 2
Student Background Characteristics and Precollege Experiences

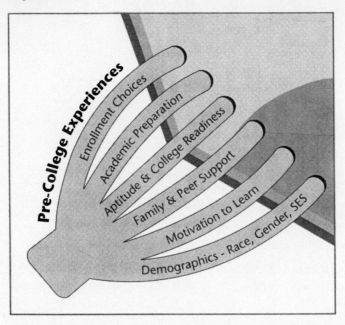

Gender

The numbers of male and female undergraduates were roughly equal from 1900 to 1930. As a result of the GI bill, male enrollments jumped dramatically following World War II so that by 1947, men outnumbered women 2.3 to 1 (Goldin, Katz, and Kuziemko, 2006). Since then, women have been gaining on men. Between 1959 and 2002, the college participation rate of women increased from 39 percent to 68 percent, a jump of 29 percent, while the proportion of men going on to college increased by only about 8 percent, from 54 percent to 62 percent (Mortenson, 2003). During this same period, the percentage of women high school graduates grew more than the percentage of male high school graduates (84 percent versus 80 percent) (Mortenson, 2003). In terms of degree completion, in 1970 men received a majority of bachelor's degrees in all fifty states, a trend that tipped in the opposite direction in 2001, when women earned a majority of such degrees (Mortenson, 2003). One reason more women than men are enrolling in college is that women outperform men on the proximate determinants of college attendance—high school grades, test scores, and college preparatory coursework. Women made especially striking gains since 1972 in terms of achievement test scores (widening their advantage in reading and narrowing the gap in mathematics) and in taking high school math and science courses. These factors, coupled with changing societal attitudes toward the role of women in the workplace and marriage and relatively greater economic benefits of college for females, appear to contribute to the larger number of women attending college.

Race and Ethnicity

Large differences exist at every grade level between whites and blacks and whites and Latinos in terms of being ready for college, with no narrowing of these gaps from 1990 to 2000 (Braswell and others, 2001). Only 21 percent of African American high school graduates, 33 percent of Hispanics, and 33 percent of students from families with annual incomes below $30,000 have college-level reading skills (American College Testing Program, 2006). Underrepresented populations have lower odds of completing high school and enrolling in college (Carter and Wilson, 1997; Social Science Research Council Project, 2005). The high school completion rates of African Americans (77 percent) and Latinos (57 percent) trailed whites (82 percent). Latino and African American college participation rates were equal at 35 percent, whereas the white participation rate was 43 percent (Carter and Wilson, 1997). If these trends continue, educational attainment in the United States could actually decline over the next fifteen years if we cannot close the gap between education levels of whites and other racial and ethnic populations (National Center for Public Policy and Higher Education, 2005).

The gender, race, and ethnicity differences in college participation and completion are more pronounced when examined by socioeconomic status. White upper- and middle-class men achieved similar academic attainment as women of similar race and SES (King, 2000). In contrast among lower-income students, only 7 percent of African American males compared with 17 percent of females and 11 percent of white males compared with 14 percent of females completed the "New Basics" high school curriculum. Moreover, all low-SES high school graduating men, regardless of race, were less likely to immediately enroll in postsecondary education (white males 25 percent versus females 35 percent, African American males 32 percent versus females 51 percent, Hispanic males 45 percent versus females 51 percent, and Asian American males 59 percent versus females 75 percent). The greater high school dropout and noncompletion rates among African American and Hispanic males compared with their similar race female counterparts may also contribute to this phenomenon. Hamrick and Stage (2004) discovered a similar gender disparity when investigating college predisposition among ethnically and racially similar eighth graders who attended high-minority, low-income schools. African American females were significantly more likely to earn higher grades, which affected parental expectations for college and directly influenced students' college predisposition. Likewise, white females were more likely to have parents who expected their child to attend college, which was the strongest predictor among white eighth graders' predisposition to college. These pronounced differences in attainment among men of color and students of moderate or economically disadvantaged means warrant further study (King, 2000).

Socioeconomic Status

Rigorous academic preparation, high educational aspirations, and family support are easier to come by if the family has economic resources. Put another way, the chances that a student will enjoy these advantages increase as family income increases, because family SES sets the stage for students' academic performance by directly providing resources at home and indirectly providing the social capital necessary to succeed in school (Coleman, 1988). Family SES determines the kind of school and classroom environment to which the student has access (Reynolds and Walberg, 1992), because nearly half of all public school funding comes from property taxes, the most important determinant of school financing (National Research Council, 1999). Although states compensate districts with limited local funds, this outside financial support often fails to create financial equity between school districts. In a nationwide study of more than seventeen thousand school districts, Parrish, Matsumoto, and Fowler (1995) found that higher neighborhood SES, as measured by the value of owner-occupied housing or by residents' educational attainment, is significantly related to greater school expenditures per student. Wenglinsky (1998) compared low SES schools with higher SES schools and found several important differences in terms of instructional arrangements, materials, teacher experience, and teacher-student ratios. In addition to the quality of instruction, family SES also influences the quality of the relationship between school personnel and parents (Watkins, 1997). Demonstrating the long-term impact of income on college student success, Astin (1993a) found that students' SES was the best predictor of earning a bachelor's degree after controlling for academic ability.

In 1996, high school completers from low-income families (bottom 20 percent SES) were less likely to attend a two- or four-year college or university immediately after high school (49 percent) than peers from middle-income (63 percent) and high-income (78 percent) families (Choy, 1999). The income level gaps between those who do and do not go to college are as wide today as they were three decades ago. In fact, some argue that low-income students may be worse off if they go to college because they are less likely to earn a degree yet will still have to repay student loans (Gladieux and Swail, 1998).

The higher the family income, the more likely it is that a student will aspire to earn a bachelor's degree, intend to enroll in college, complete an application, and gain college admission. SES also dictates high school students' curricular preparation for college. In 1992, 53 percent of low-income children (from families earning less than $25,000) were qualified for college, compared with 68 percent of middle-income children ($25,000 to $74,999) and 86 percent of high-income children (more than $75,000) (Choy, 1999). Further illustrating this point, middle-income Latinos had a 17 percent higher probability of earning a bachelor's degree compared with low-income Latinos (Swail, Cabrera, Lee, and Williams, 2005). Unfortunately, higher economic need is concentrated in populations already underrepresented in postsecondary education. For example, Latino eighth graders were more likely to have low-income backgrounds; 46 percent had family incomes less than $25,000, compared with 17 percent of white children (Swail, Cabrera, Lee, and Williams, 2005).

Where a student enrolls is also related to family income. For example, low-income high school graduates who were academically qualified and took steps necessary for admission were less likely than high-income students to enroll in a four-year institution (83 percent versus 92 percent) (Choy, 1999). Students with family incomes of $60,000 or more were less likely to enroll in public two-year institutions (34 percent) than students with family incomes between $30,000 and $59,999 (47 percent) and students with family incomes of less than $30,000 (43 percent) (Choy, 1999). Among 1992 high school seniors in the highest achievement test quartile, students whose families were also in the highest SES quartile were considerably more likely than those in the lowest SES quartile to attend a four-year college within two years of graduating from high school (86 percent versus 56 percent) (Choy, 1999).

Financial Aid

Since 1990, the number of students attending college with unmet financial need has increased dramatically (National Center for Public Policy and Higher Education, 2002), which is not surprising given the rising costs in tuition and related college expenses described earlier. In 1995–96, the average net price of full-time undergraduate enrollment was $5,700 at public two-year institutions (price minus aid for a dependent), $7,300 at public four-year colleges, and $11,200 at private, not-for-profit institutions (Choy, 1999). The average unmet need (net price minus expected family contribution and financial aid) for low-income full-time undergraduate enrollment at public four-year institutions was about $3,800, and the average unmet need at private, not-for-profit four-year institutions was $6,200 (Choy, 1999). These figures are important to consider in light of the total family expected contribution to students' educational expenses.

Among a sample of full-time dependent undergraduates enrolled during 1995–96, 35 percent were lower income ($34,999 or below), 37 percent were middle income ($35,000 to $69,999), and 28 percent were higher income ($70,000) (Presley and Clery, 2001). Almost all low-income students (99 percent) had some financial need compared with 79 percent of middle-income students and 33 percent of high-income students (Presley and Clery, 2001). Further, 87 percent of low-income students had unmet financial need, which was on average $4,915, and close to three times their average expected family contribution ($1,617). This unmet financial need was considerably greater than that of middle-income students. The financial challenges of attending a four-year school compared with enrolling in a two-year community college and living at home may make matriculation at such institutions unrealistic for low-income students and may also explain why highly qualified lower SES students were less interested in attending four-year institutions as tuition and distance from home increased (National Center for Public Policy and Higher Education, 2002), demonstrating how the availability and type of financial aid can affect students' college attendance and their persistence (Gladieux and Swail, 1998).

Financial aid appears to play different roles in promoting student success based on its source and student SES. A substantially higher proportion of students, especially those from middle-income families, receive financial aid at private, not-for-profit four-year institutions than any other institutional type (National Center for Public Policy and Higher Education, 2002)—suggesting that institutional aid may primarily function to promote choice for private, not-for-profit four-year institutions, which tend to be most expensive (National Center for Public Policy and Higher Education, 2002). Federal need-based financial aid is expected to foster student access because calculated need increases as family ability to pay decreases; it is also expected to encourage student choice because need increases as a student's price of attendance increases.

Academic preparation and applying to college appear to be more important than socioeconomic status in choosing a college. Berkner and Chavez (1997) found that among 1,988 eighth graders who graduated from high school, low-income students were able to attend four-year colleges at the same rate as students from middle-income families *if* they became qualified for college by taking college prep classes, entrance exams, and applying to college. College-qualified low-income students who were accepted for admission to public and private four-year institutions were just as likely to enroll as middle- and upper-income students (Berkner and Chavez, 1997). On the other hand, low SES and minority students were less likely to take those steps and therefore less likely overall to enroll in four-year institutions (National Center for Public Policy and Higher Education, 2002).

Gift aid in the form of scholarships and grants and work-study programs (as contrasted with loans) are associated with higher retention and graduate rates (Pell Institute, 2004), especially for low-income and minority students (St. John, 2002; Swail with Redd and Perna, 2003). Grants have a strong effect on low-income and minority student performance. For example, African American students are highly sensitive to college costs in terms of choosing and persisting in college (St. John, Paulsen, and Carter, 2005). At the same time, the African American population exhibits considerable economic diversity, so SES is a key factor. Loans seem to be more effective for whites, though they are also price sensitive because of the great range in family income. Providing an African American or Hispanic student with an additional $1,000 in grant funds decreased the probability of dropping out by 7 percent and 8 percent, respectively (General Accounting Office, 1995). Loans are associated with higher persistence rates only for white students (General Accounting Office, 1995). Other institutional policies to improve time to degree rates combine financial assistance and course scheduling benefits such as "four-year completion guarantees" (that is, ensuring courses needed to graduate will be available during a four-year period) (Illinois State Board of Higher Education, 2003).

Although working and going to school are sometimes competing goals, limited on- or off-campus work does not appear to seriously inhibit student success (Pascarella, 2001). Among students seeking a bachelor's or associate's degree who considered themselves primarily students working to pay their expenses, those who worked fifteen or fewer hours were more likely than students who worked more to attend for the full year, suggesting that working more than fifteen hours may negatively affect persistence (Choy, 1999). On-campus or work-study employment is more often associated with student success, as working on campus provides a channel of communication to students and helps students use the educational system effectively (Institute for Higher Education Policy, 2001; Kuh, Kinzie, Schuh, Whitt, and Associates, 2005) and also is linked with higher transfer rates for community college students (Turner, 1988). Work-study positions for students in the third year of study and beyond are particularly beneficial to student persistence and learning when the positions are aligned with students' academic interests and career goals (Institute for Higher Education Policy, 2001).

Unmet financial need and insufficient amounts of institutional aid provided by public institutions, however, may force students to work considerable hours to finance their college education. In 1995–96 among undergraduates who considered themselves primarily students working to pay for college expenses, the more time students worked the more likely they reported that employment limited class schedules, reduced choices of classes, and limited the number of courses taken (Heller, 2002). Those who worked full time (35 hours or more) while enrolled at least half time reported all these negative effects (Heller, 2002). Reducing weekly employment hours diminishes the negative effects of working, indicating that a modest amount of work is positively related with full-time enrollment, enhanced self-esteem (Gleason, 1993), integration in the campus environment (Murdock, 1990), and persistence (Heller, 2002; Pascarella and others, 1998).

Family and Peer Support

Another major factor in influencing a student's likely educational trajectory is one's family and friends. As we shall see, these people play an important role in shaping aspirations and reinforcing behaviors consistent with academic achievement.

Family Educational Background

In addition to race, ethnicity, and socioeconomic background, parental education also affects students' educational aspirations (Hamrick and Stage, 2004). In fact, parental education is an important variable for predicting college predisposition among all low SES students, but the strength of this relationship depends on students' race and gender rather than having the same effects for all.

Approximately one in three college students comes from families where neither parent had any postsecondary education (National Survey of Student Engagement, 2005). First-generation students are more likely to be female, to be older, to have lower incomes, to be married, and to have dependents (Nuñez and Cuccaro-Alamin, 1998). Racial and ethnic minority groups are also disproportionately represented among first-generation students, with Latino students being most heavily represented (Nuñez and Cuccaro-Alamin,

1998; Warburton, Bugarin, and Nuñez, 2001). More than two-fifths (42 percent) of Latino students had parents whose highest level of education was less than high school, contrasted with only 18 percent of whites (Swail, Cabrera, Lee, and Williams, 2005).

Enrollment and graduation rates suggest that the odds are stacked against first-generation students' succeeding in college (Baum and Payea, 2004). For example, in 1996 high school completers' enrollment rates in postsecondary education ranged from 45 percent for those with parents who had less than a high school education to 85 percent for those students with parents with a bachelor's degree or higher (Choy, 1999). First-generation students were less likely to take advanced math and advance placement classes, were less knowledgeable about how to apply for college and financial aid, had lower grades, and were less engaged overall in high school (High School Survey of Student Engagement, 2005; Terenzini and others, 1996). Forty percent of first-generation students score in the lowest quartile of the American College Test (ACT) or Scholastic Aptitude Test (SAT) (Choy, 1999). They are also more likely to enroll at public universities and attend part time (Choy, 1999) and are twice as likely to take remedial courses (21 percent versus 10 percent) after controlling for high school rigor (Warburton, Bugarin, and Nuñez, 2001).

First-generation students and students from the lowest income quartile are also less likely to transfer to four-year institutions (Bailey and others, 2005). Cejda and Kaylor (2001) found that faculty encouragement is a strong positive influence on whether community college students transfer, and many students do not intend to do so until encouraged by faculty members and, to a lesser degree, by peers. Institutional barriers such as the difficulty of transferring credits appear to preclude students from transferring.

Although Billson and Terry (1982) found no differences in the educational aspirations of first- and second-generation students, more recently Terenzini and others (1996) reported that first-generation students had lower educational aspirations than their second-generation counterparts. Students whose fathers completed college were three times more likely than their classmates to indicate that achieving a college degree was their educational goal; respondents whose mothers completed college were twice as likely (McCarthy and

Kuh, 2006). Among African American and Latina eighth graders in low-income minority schools, parental college education had a direct positive influence on students' predisposition to attend college. For Hispanic male and white students in similar school environments, however, parental college education had only indirect positive effects. For Hispanic males, parental education directly influenced parents' expectations for their child's college attendance, which had a significant positive effect on students' predispositions to college. For white students, parental college education had a significant positive influence on parents' expectations for college and composite grades, which positively influenced students' college aspirations.

On balance, even after controlling for socioeconomic status, institution type, and enrollment patterns, first-generation status still has a negative effect on degree completion. In fact, "students whose parents held a bachelor's degree or higher were five times more likely to earn a bachelor's degree than were similar first-generation students (50 percent versus 11 percent)" (Pascarella and Terenzini, 2005, p. 590).

The priorities of first-generation students are also different. They are, for example, more likely to want to be well off financially (Nuñez and Cuccaro-Alamin, 1998). Their choice of educational institutions is also more heavily influenced by the nature and amount of financial aid, perceptions of the amount of homework required, and being able to live at home and to work while going to school. They are also more likely to delay enrollment after high school, attend two-year institutions, attend part time and work full time, and live off campus, all of which contribute to their being less likely to get involved with campus organizations and to have more difficulty adjusting to college (Choy, 2001; Pascarella, Pierson, Wolniak, and Terenzini, 2004; Pike and Kuh, 2005a; Richardson and Skinner, 1992; Terenzini and others, 1994, 1996; Tym McMillion, Barone, and Webster, 2004; Warburton, Bugarin, and Nuñez, 2001). Managing college tuition costs may underlie these decisions, as working during college is not a choice but a means of survival for many first-generation students. As a result, they are less likely to finish their degrees in five years—if they finish.

If these obstacles were not enough, first-generation students typically have less-well-developed time management and other personal skills, less family and social support for attending college, less knowledge about higher education, and less experience navigating bureaucratic institutions (Attinasi, 1989; London, 1989; Nuñez and Cuccaro-Alamin, 1998; Terenzini and others, 1996; York-Anderson and Bowman, 1991). Students who enter a college environment where the predominant racial, ethnic, or religious culture differs from their own may encounter an additional set of adjustment challenges (Allen, 1992); these dynamics are to a certain degree similar for first-generation, low-income white students because of their low socioeconomic status. For this host of reasons, it is no wonder first-generation college students are more likely to drop out (73 percent to 60 percent) or to stop out of college for a period of time (19 percent to 8 percent) (Warburton, Bugarin, and Nuñez, 2001).

First-generation status also has a negative influence on pursuing a doctoral degree (Chen, 2005). African American males and females remain underrepresented in most doctoral programs, especially in the sciences and engineering (Solorzano, 1995). Students' chances of obtaining a postbaccalaureate degree appear to be enhanced by interactions with faculty, academic achievement, and academic involvement (Fischer, 1995; Pascarella and Terenzini, 2005).

Educational Aspirations and Family Support

Aspirations and family support foreshadow student success (Perna and Titus, 2005). Planning for college and postsecondary activities as early as the eighth grade increases the prospects for completing college (Swail, Cabrera, Lee, and Williams, 2005). In fact, parental expectations were the strongest predictor of predisposition to college among white eighth graders who attended low-income, high-minority schools (Hamrick and Stage, 2004). Naumann, Bandalos, and Gutkin (2003) found that for first-generation students, educational aspirations were the best predictor of first semester grade point average (GPA). Although the overwhelming majority (97 percent) of students of all races expect to enroll in some form of postsecondary education, many do not follow through (U.S. Department of Education, 2003a). Only 60 percent take the minimum coursework recommended for college (Venezia, Kirst, and Antonio, 2003). High school teachers may diminish students' aspirations, as teachers' expectations for their students were lower than those of parents and students themselves. Many teachers apparently believe that certain groups of students are limited in what and how much they can learn, and they lower their performance expectations for these students (U.S. Department of Education, 2004).

Studies of the influence of Latino students' educational aspirations have resulted in mixed findings. One study showed that Latino parents of high school seniors place nearly twice as much emphasis on the necessity of a college education for success compared with African American and white parents. Even so, the reality of participation falls far short of the expectation (Immerwahr, 2000). Another study showed that Latino parents were less likely to have postsecondary expectations for their children, with less than three-fifths (58 percent) expecting their children to go to college, compared with more than four-fifths (82 percent) of white parents. Similarly, more white students (79 percent) aspired to a postsecondary degree, compared with Latinos (63 percent) (Swail, Cabrera, Lee, and Williams, 2005). Regardless of whether it occurs less frequently, parents' expectations are a strong direct indicator of Latino eighth graders' predispositions for college, particularly among students at low-income, high-minority schools (Hamrick and Stage, 2004).

Parents and peers seem to influence both student enrollment (Perna and Titus, 2005) and persistence decisions (Bank, Slavings, and Biddle, 1990), though African American students apparently benefit less than others from conversations with their parents about college (Perna and Titus, 2005). In a related finding, the parents of African American eighth graders who attended low-income, high-minority schools had higher expectations for college attendance when their children achieved high grades as well as participated in cocurricular activities (Hamrick and Stage, 2004). It may be that parental encouragement hinges on these prerequisite student achievements and behaviors under certain environmental conditions and challenges. On balance, it appears that students perform better and are more likely to succeed when their families affirm their choices and encourage them to persevere, especially for underserved populations (Gutierrez, 2000; Pathways to College Network, 2004; Tierney, Corwin, and Colyar, 2005). Thus an appropriate amount of parental involvement and support can help offset negative impacts of poverty to a degree (Chrispeels and Rivero, 2001).

Academic Preparation and Motivation to Learn

What students study in high school, especially the rigor of classes, establishes a foundation for their postsecondary academic performance. Similarly, what students expect to happen in college shapes to a certain degree what they subsequently do.

Academic Intensity in High School

The quality of the academic experience and intensity of the high school curriculum affect almost every dimension of success in postsecondary education, suggesting that a rigorous high school curriculum can narrow the college persistence gap (Nuñez and Cuccaro-Alamin, 1998; Warburton, Bugarin, and Nuñez, 2001). Those students best prepared coming out of high school also are best positioned to do well in college, regardless of who they are, how much money they have, or where they go to college (Florida Department of Education, 2005; Gladieux and Swail, 1998, Horn and Kojaku, 2001; Martinez and Klopott, 2003; Warburton, Bugarin, and Nuñez, 2001). First-generation students, for example, perform pretty much like other students in terms of their college grades (3.0 to 3.1 GPA) and remedial coursework (only 4 to 5 percent take such courses).

High school grades are the strongest predictor of first-year college grades, accounting for 25 to 33 percent of the variance (Pike and Saupe, 2002). About nine of ten (87 percent) students who complete four years of math, science, and English in high school stay on track to graduate from college, compared with a 62 percent persistence rate among those who do not complete that coursework (Adelman, 1999; Warburton, Bugarin, and Nuñez, 2001). Although completing high-level mathematics classes in high school—algebra II, precalculus, trigonometry, calculus—is the single best high school predictor of performing well academically in college (Adelman, 1999, 2006), such opportunities are not equally distributed. For example, Latino students and those from any SES quintile other than the highest are less likely to attend high schools that offer calculus. Thus the course-taking patterns of Latinos are concentrated in classes below algebra II (46 percent), whereas those of whites are concentrated at algebra II and trigonometry (45 percent). At the highest math levels, 27 percent of whites took precalculus and calculus, compared with only

15 percent of Latinos. Swail, Cabrera, Lee, and Williams (2005) found that taking precalculus and calculus increased Latinos' chances of college completion by 12 percent. These low participation rates may explain why college dropout rates of certain racial, ethnic, and socioeconomic groups remain relatively high.

African American students are more likely to attend public high schools with high minority concentrations from low socioeconomic communities (Hoffman, Llagas, and Snyder, 2003) and were less likely than white students to take advanced mathematics and science courses and less likely than white or Hispanic students to take advanced placement exams. According to O'Brien and Zudak (1998), segregated neighborhoods usually equate to inferior resources, which eventually results in inferior levels of education for minority groups. Gonzalez, Cauce, Friedman, and Mason (1996) further supported this finding by examining the combined effect of family and neighborhood influences on the school performance of African American high school students. They found that family SES was less predictive of academic achievement compared with neighborhood SES factors. Neighborhood factors related to lower grades and moderated parenting support, which may be the result of having financially weaker neighborhood schools that struggle to attract and keep qualified teachers (Wenglinsky, 1998), an issue addressed again in the discussion of socioeconomic status.

Expectations for College

Understanding what students expect of and from their college experience is crucial for institutions to fashion policies and practices that effectively address students' learning needs (Miller and others, 2005). When students' expectations and experiences are appropriately aligned and match the reality they encounter, students are more likely to be satisfied with their college experience and to persist to graduation, a happy outcome for both students and institutions (Braxton, Vesper, and Hossler, 1995). But as Schilling and Schilling (1999) concluded from their analysis of College Student Expectations Questionnaire results, many students enter college with uninformed expectations that diverge substantially from those of the faculty. Substantial numbers of traditional-age students start college "disengaged" from the learning process, having acquired a cumulative deficit in terms of attitudes, study habits, and academic skills (Levine and Cureton, 1998; McCarthy and Kuh, 2006; Marchese, 1997, 1998; National Survey of Student Engagement, 2005). For example, in the mid-1990s high school seniors reported studying only about six hours per week on average, well below the amount traditionally assumed necessary to do well in college. More recent studies (McCarthy and Kuh, 2006) show similar findings. Compared with their counterparts of a decade earlier, high school seniors were more frequently bored in class and missed more classes as a result of oversleeping or other obligations (Sax and others, 2003). Even so, record numbers reported B+ or better high school grades and expected to earn at least a B average in college. Because behavioral patterns established in elementary and secondary school tend to persist through the college years (Schilling and Schilling, 1999), we should not be surprised that the majority of first-year students—about 70 percent—report working just hard enough to get by (National Survey of Student Engagement).

Another reason it is important to learn more about the degree to which college expectations and experiences are congruent is that first-generation students pursuing higher education have less tacit knowledge about what college is like. As a result, if their perceptions and expectations are off the mark, they will be less well prepared to deal with the challenges they encounter, which will make it more difficult to perform well academically, adjust socially, and persist to graduation.

Assuming many students matriculate with an entitlement mentality, what they expect to do in college and what faculty members and postsecondary institutions provide could result in a problematic mismatch of sizable proportion, a potentially debilitating condition in light of the theoretical perspectives on student success reviewed in "Major Theoretical Perspectives on Student Success in College." This mismatch arises because expectations can be a psychological catalyst or a deterrent to certain types of behavior, serving as a filter through which students compare what is unfolding with what they think should happen and decide whether certain activities are appropriate, meaningful, relevant, and worth their time, and what opportunities and activities to ignore (Bandura, 1982; Cantor and Mischel, 1977; Dweck and Leggett, 1988; Feldman, 1981; Snyder and Swann, 1978). For example, if a student does not expect to do research with a faculty member, take part in cultural events, or study abroad, chances are that opportunities to pursue these activities will be overlooked or dismissed out of hand. Expectations therefore shape subsequent behaviors and experiences (Feldman, 1981).

Student background characteristics and precollege experiences shape expectations to varying degrees. For example, Olsen and others (1998) found that students with strong academic high school records were more likely to get involved in a range of activities during college. Student demographic and background characteristics had small, almost negligible effects on their collegiate experiences and outcomes. Students whose expectations for college were relatively low were more likely to report college experiences congruent with those low expectations, compared with students with relatively high expectations. Finally, those students who indicated a desire to participate in a wide range of intellectual, social, and cultural activities during the first year of college were more likely to do so, compared with others whose expectations were more narrowly defined. As a result of their somewhat broader range of interests, these students also were more likely to subsequently participate in activities that are predictors of academic success and persistence.

Whether students' expectations for college are well enough formed to be reliable predictors of persistence and success is a legitimate question (Pascarella and Terenzini, 2005) that awaits a definitive empirical answer. Studies over the past several decades suggest that students have a fair understanding of many of the aspects of what they will experience in the first year of college. Students appear to be reasonably accurate in terms of how they will manage the transition to college (Baker, McNeil, and Siryk, 1985; Berdie, 1966, 1968; Stern, 1970; Whiteley, 1982), though some of it may be a function of self-fulfilling prophecy (Merton, 1948). Therefore, in the absence of unequivocal information to the contrary, it seems prudent to learn more about the relationships between what students expect and what they put into and get out of their college experience.

One area where students' expectations are less accurate is related to estimating what the campus environment will be like. Braxton, Vesper, and Hossler (1995) found that first-generation students' expectations about the college environment were less congruent with what they actually experienced. And there is evidence that what students actually do in the first year of college falls short of what they expected to do in many areas (Kuh, 1999; Kuh, Gonyea, and

Williams, 2005; Olsen and others, 1998). That is, when starting out, most first-year students say they will engage in more academic and other educationally purposeful activities more frequently than they actually reported doing near the end of the first year. Though students may be somewhat idealistic in terms of what they can accomplish during college, some of their expectations are not unrealistic, at least when compared with the amount of reading and writing that faculty members assert is appropriate and some other important activities. For example, two-thirds think they will become acquainted with students from racial and ethnic backgrounds different from their own, but substantially fewer have "frequent" substantive discussions with such people during the first year (42 percent). A fifth "never" had such discussions, about four times the number (5 percent) who thought they would not do so when starting college.

Virtually everyone agrees that student-faculty interaction is an important factor in student success (for example, Astin, 1993b; Kuh and others, 1991; Pascarella and Terenzini, 1991; Tinto, 1993), and entering college students think so too. For example, 94 percent say they will at least occasionally ask their instructor about their performance. Less than two-thirds actually do so, however (Kuh, 2005). The majority (69 percent) expect to socialize at least "occasionally" with faculty members outside the classroom, but only about two-fifths (41 percent) report doing so. More than three-quarters (77 percent) expect that they will "frequently" ask their teachers for information about the course (assignments and such), but only about half (54 percent) do so. Perhaps the difference is that students are not certain how often they will need to ask faculty members for information, so they err on the high side. The discrepancy between what students expect and experience in terms of interacting with faculty may also be partly the result of reward systems and large first-year classes that discourage such contacts.

The expected and reported levels of engagement vary by certain student characteristics and in predictable ways by institutional type (Astin, 1993b; Gonyea, 2005; Pace, 1990). For example, women expect to engage more frequently in educationally purposeful activities than men. And they do, except for recreational sports and science-related activities. As with women, students of color expect to more frequently participate in a range of educationally purposeful activities. They expect to have more interactions with students from different backgrounds than they subsequently experience. Students at smaller selective colleges have greater expectations across the board, and they subsequently report being involved to a greater extent in more activities during college. They also, on average, expect and find their campus environments to be more supportive. As we shall see in the next section, however, some large schools outperform some small schools on these and other dimensions (Kuh, 2001, 2003; National Survey of Student Engagement, 2005).

Enrollment Choices and Patterns

Where and when students choose to go to college can affect the odds that they will earn a credential or degree. The upwards of three-quarters of high school graduates who eventually go on to some form of postsecondary education sort themselves into five types of institutions: two-year colleges (46 percent), public four-year colleges (26 percent), private four-year colleges (15 percent), for-profit entities (10 percent), and other types of schools (3 percent).

The research consistently shows that delaying postsecondary enrollment, for whatever reason, reduces the odds that the student will persist and complete a degree program (Adelman, 2006b). Indeed, Exhibit 1 shows that delayed entry is one of the seven major risk factors that threaten persistence and graduation (Berkner, Cuccaro-Alamin, and McCormick, 1996; Carroll, 1989; Horn and Premo, 1995; McCormick and Horn, 1996). Students with two or more of these characteristics are more likely to drop out than their peers (Choy, 2001; Muraskin and Lee, with Wilner and Swail, 2004; State Higher Education Executive Officers, 2005; Swail with Redd and Perna, 2003).

The conditions associated with premature departure from college partially explain the low baccalaureate attainment rates of certain groups of students, among them community college students and many ethnic minorities. For example, almost 50 percent of all first-time community college students (and in some settings significantly more) are assessed as underprepared for the academic demands of college-level work. And it is another major reason that about half of community college students do not return to college for their second year of studies (Community College Survey of Student Engagement, 2005). Just over half of Latino students attended postsecondary institutions part

EXHIBIT 1
Risk Factors That Threaten Persistence and Graduation from College

- Being academically underprepared for college-level work
- Not entering college directly after high school
- Attending college part-time
- Being a single parent
- Being financially independent (students who rely on their own income or savings and whose parents are not sources of income for meeting college costs)
- Caring for children at home
- Working more than thirty hours per week
- Being a first-generation college student

Source: Community College Survey of Student Engagement, 2005.

time (52 percent), compared with 37 percent of white students. Although nearly two-thirds (64 percent) of whites attended postsecondary institutions continuously, only two-fifths of Latinos attended postsecondary institutions without stopping out (Swail, Cabrera, Lee, and Williams, 2005). Latinos were more likely to delay enrollment to postsecondary education, as 77 percent of Latinos (compared with 82 percent of whites) entered postsecondary education within seven months of graduating from high school. In addition, African American and Hispanic community college students are also less likely to earn baccalaureate degrees because they are overrepresented in certificate programs (Bailey and others, 2005). Attending a tribal college seems to have a positive impact on encouraging Native American community college graduates to pursue baccalaureate degrees (American Indian Higher Education Consortium, Institute for Higher Education Policy, and Sallie Mae Education Institute, 2000).

Two-year colleges have either a "warming" (more likely to earn a degree— Swanson, 2002) or "cooling" (more likely to drop out of college—Pascarella and others, 1998; McCormick, 1990; 1997) effect, depending on the comparison group (Pascarella and Terenzini, 2005). That is, full-time enrollment at a two-year college increases one's chances of earning a baccalaureate degree, compared with students who never enrolled in postsecondary education, but students who initially enroll at a four-year college are more likely to graduate compared with their counterparts who start at a two-year college. In large part, it is because two-year colleges enroll a disproportionate number of high-risk students who exhibit several of the risk factors shown in Exhibit 1. In fact, students attending community colleges are *three to four times more likely* than their counterparts in four-year colleges and universities to reflect four or more of these risk factors (Community College Survey of Student Engagement, 2005). For example, more than half (55 percent) of nontraditional-age women attending two-year colleges, compared with only 15 percent of their counterparts, spend more than thirty hours per week caring for dependents who live with them. Yet twice as many nontraditional-age women in two-year colleges spend more than twenty-one hours per week studying (13 percent nontraditional age and 6 percent traditional age)!

In addition, interruptions in enrollment can also reduce one's chances of earning a degree. According to Pascarella and Terenzini (2005, p. 381), "'Stopping-out' not only increases time-to-degree, but also reduces the likelihood of degree completion, whether an associate or baccalaureate degree (Carroll, 1989; Ganderton and Santos, 1995; Guerin, 1997; Hanniford and Sagoria, 1994; Horn, 1998; Porter, 1990). Even transferring from one four-year institution to another reduces the odds of degree completion. Among students beginning at a four-year college or university, those who do not transfer are significantly more likely to earn their bachelor's degrees in five years than are 'horizontal' transfers who move to another four-year school (McCormick, 1997)."

An increasingly common pattern is attending two or more institutions—sometimes two or more during the same academic term—on the road to the baccalaureate degree without any definitive pattern of type of institution attended (Adelman, 2006b). Sometimes called "swirl" (de los Santos and Wright, 1990; Borden, 2004), this meandering from one institution to another (Adelman, 2006b) can include coenrollment (attending more than one institution simultaneously, also called "overlapping enrollment" or "dual enrollment") and attending another institution without transferring from the first institution (Borden, 2004).

Understanding the dynamics and consequences of swirl is not just an academic exercise, given that nearly three-fifths of students from the 1992 high school graduating class who earned a baccalaureate degree by December 2002 attended more than one institution. More than a third (35 percent) attended more than two colleges or universities. Even among 1999–2000 bachelor's degree recipients who started college at a four-year institution, about 47 percent had attended another institution at some point with or without transferring (Adelman, 2006b). More important, while transferring from one college to another (whether from a two-year school to a four-year institution or vice versa) is positively related to degree completion, swirling is not (Adelman, 2006b; see also Peter and Cataldi, 2005). In addition, swirling appears to dampen student engagement, as shown later in this report.

Summary

The major themes from this section underscore the complex ways that student background characteristics and precollege experiences interact to influence enrollment patterns and, subsequently, student success.

The quality of high school academic preparation strongly predicts chances for postsecondary success, measured by enrollment, persistence, grades, and educational attainment.

Family education background is related to students' higher postsecondary aspirations and greater likelihood of enrollment, persistence, and attainment.

Socioeconomic status influences prior academic preparation, pursuing steps to postsecondary enrollment and admission, enrollment, and degree completion.

The availability and type of financial aid significantly affects students' college attendance and persistence.

Enrollment patterns (full time or part time, two-year or four-year institution, direct or delayed enrollment) all influence students' long term attainment and success.

Understanding what the factors are and how they work together provides information that various groups can use to help better prepare students for collegiate and postcollegiate success. Students from at-risk populations face additional challenges, some of which can be ameliorated by the activities in which they engage in college and the programs and practices institutions provided for their enrichment.

Student Behaviors, Activities, and Experiences Associated with Student Success

A S DEMONSTRATED IN THE PREVIOUS CHAPTER, student characteristics and their precollege experiences influence to a nontrivial extent whether students will enroll in postsecondary education, how they will perform academically, and whether they will persist and attain their educational objectives. In fact, the best predictor of college grades is the combination of an individual student's academic preparation, high school grades, aspirations, and motivation.

Once students start college, another key factor in their success—broadly defined—is "student engagement," or the extent to which they take part in educationally effective practices. In their landmark publication, "Seven Principles for Good Practice in Undergraduate Education," Chickering and Gamson (1987) underscored seven categories of effective educational practices that directly influence student learning and the quality of their educational experiences: student-faculty contact, cooperation among students, active learning, prompt feedback, time on task, high expectations, and respect for diverse talents and ways of learning. Generally speaking, the more students engage in these kinds of activities, the more they learn and the more likely they are to persist and graduate from college.[1]

At institutions where faculty members use these and other effective educational practices more frequently in their classes, students are more engaged overall and gain more from college (Pascarella and Terenzini, 2005). Thus the nature and quality of first-year students' experiences in the classroom, with faculty, and with peers are better predictors of desired educational outcomes associated with college attendance than precollege characteristics (Gerken and Volkwien, 2000).

Also important to student learning are institutional environments that are perceived by students to be inclusive and affirming where expectations for performance are clearly communicated and set at reasonably high levels (Education Commission of the States, 1995; Kuh, 2001; Kuh, Kinzie, Schuh, Whitt, and Associates, 2005; Kuh and others, 1991; Pascarella, 2001).

Student engagement represents two critical features. The first is the amount of time and effort students put into their studies and other educationally purposeful activities. "Learning is strongly influenced by the degree to which an individual is invested in the learning process" (Alexander and Murphy, 1994, p. 12). The second component of student engagement is how the institution deploys its resources and organizes the curriculum, other learning opportunities, and support services to induce students to participate in activities that lead to the experiences and desired outcomes such as persistence, satisfaction, learning, and graduation (Kuh, 2001). As Pascarella and Terenzini (2005, p. 602) concluded, "The impact of college is largely determined by individual effort and involvement in the academic, interpersonal, and extracurricular offerings on a campus ..."

As depicted in the top left portion of Figure 3, this section reviews research on the aspects of student engagement focusing on student behaviors—what

FIGURE 3
Student Behaviors and Student Engagement

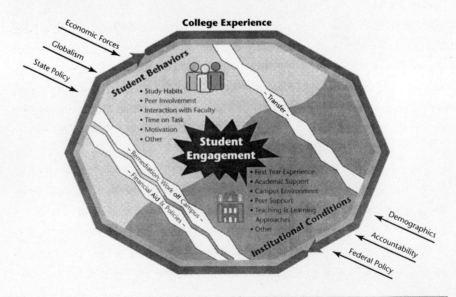

students do with an institution's resources for learning. As in previous sections, we are especially interested in what the literature offers in terms of the relationships between engagement and success in college for students who may be at risk of premature departure or underperformance—first-generation students, transfers, and students from historically underserved backgrounds.

College Activities

The College Student Expectations Questionnaire, the National Survey of Student Engagement (NSSE), and the Community College Survey of Student Engagement (CCSSE) focus primarily on students' participation in activities that are associated with desired learning outcomes, persistence, and satisfaction. The NSSE annually obtains information from four-year colleges and universities nationwide about students' participation in programs and activities that institutions provide for their learning and personal development. Survey items represent empirically confirmed "good practices" in undergraduate education. Taken together, the host of studies using these measures point to seven conclusions about student engagement as an intermediate outcome and as a proxy for student success.

Student engagement in educationally purposeful activities is positively related to both grades and persistence. Pascarella and Terenzini (2005) concluded that college grades are probably the best predictor of student persistence, degree completion, and graduate school enrollment. Good grades in the first year are especially important to subsequent academic success and degree completion, as strong academic achievement seems to reduce the chances of a student's stopping out and increases the probability of timely degree completion. For example, Adelman (1999) found that both first-year grades and trends in subsequent grades predicted bachelor's degree completion beyond the effects of other variables, including students' precollege characteristics, institutional selectivity, financial aid, hours worked, and selected college experience variables. Performing in the top two quintiles of the grade distribution improved the odds twofold that a student would complete a degree compared with his or her counterparts in the bottom three quintiles. Other studies found similar results, even when controlling for students' background characteristics and college experiences (Astin, 1993b; Heller, 2001; Horn, 1998). Undergraduate grades also have a modest positive impact on being employed full time early in one's career in a position appropriate to one's bachelor's degree. Although grades do not appear to be causally related to job satisfaction or job mobility, they do have a "positive net impact on both occupational status and earnings" (Pascarella and Terenzini, 2005, p. 619).

Student engagement is linked to a wide array of desired college outcomes, so it is no surprise that engagement and grades go hand in hand. In fact, GPA is positively related to all the effective educational practices measured by the NSSE and nearly all those represented on the CCSSE (Community College Survey of Student Engagement, 2005; National Survey of Student Engagement, 2005). Specifically for students at four-year colleges, GPA is associated with time spent preparing for class, coming to class prepared, asking questions in class, tutoring other students, receiving prompt feedback from faculty, maintaining high-quality relationships with faculty, and having a favorable evaluation of overall educational experiences in college. These patterns generally hold for both first-year and senior students, though they do not explain the direction of the relationship between grades and engagement. That is, does engagement result in higher grades, or do higher grades promote more engagement? Other findings from the NSSE over the years indicate:

Women report higher grades than men.

At both two-year and four-year colleges, white students generally reported higher grades than students of color.[2] Why students of color report lower grades for comparable academic effort is not clear.

Few students at four-year colleges report C or lower average grades, that is, only 5 percent of first-year students and 1 percent of seniors.

Grade patterns vary by major fields. Seniors majoring in education, foreign languages, humanities, math, and the visual and performing arts report the highest GPAs, while those majoring in agriculture, engineering, and public administration report the lowest.

Grades do not vary appreciably by institutional type or selectivity strata, though the *distribution* of grades is considerably compressed at more selective institutions (Hu, 2005; Kuh and Hu, 1999).

Figure 4 shows the effect of engagement (a global measure based on 19 NSSE items) on first-year college grades by precollege ability (composite ACT score). The data on which this display is based concern about sixty-two hundred students at eighteen diverse four-year colleges and universities where student records and NSSE results were matched to estimate the relationships between engagement and college grades. The regression model included a term capturing the interaction between precollege achievement and engagement. Model coefficients and the descriptive statistics for the sample were used to estimate first-year GPA for the "typical" student. It is noteworthy that the grades of lower-ability students were positively affected by engagement in educationally effective activities to a greater degree compared with higher-ability students. Thus engagement appears to have a conditional, compensatory effect on grades.

To examine the relationships between graduation rates and scores on the five NSSE clusters of effective educational practice, results from random samples of first-year students and seniors at 680 four-year institutions in 2004 and 2005

FIGURE 4
Impact of Engagement in Educationally Purposeful Activities on First-Year GPA

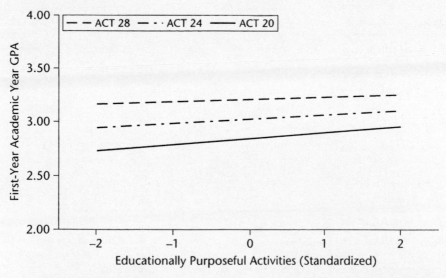

Source: First-year GPA provided by eighteen institutions with NSSE data from 2001 through 2003.

were analyzed. Table 1 shows that all but one of the correlations between the four- and six-year graduation rates and first-year student and senior NSSE benchmark scores at the institutional level are statistically significant ($p < .05$). The lone outlier is the correlation between six-year graduation rate and active and collaborative learning. In fact, all but one of the correlations (graduation and senior active and collaborative learning) are significant at $p < .001$. Eleven of the twenty correlations exceed .37, suggesting a relatively strong positive relationship between student engagement and graduation at the institutional level.

Although these results indicate strong ties between engagement and persistence, it is wise to exercise some caution when making conclusive statements because the data were collected at different points in time. The institutional graduation rates reported in 2004 were the best, most complete data available at the time; thus, the graduation rates represent

TABLE 1
Correlations Between Institutional Mean Scores of NSSE Clusters of Effective Educational Practices and Institutional Graduation Rates for 680 Four-Year Colleges and Universities

Educational Practice	First-Year Students		Seniors	
	4–Year Rate	6–Year Rate	4–Year Rate	6–Year Rate
Academic Challenge	.621***	.523***	.481***	.377***
Active and Collaborative Learning	.233***	.103***	.156***	.052
Student-Faculty Interaction	.261***	.090***	.427***	.299*
Enriching Educational Experiences	.503***	.458***	.617***	.539***
Supportive Campus Environment	.483***	.373***	.312***	.151***

Note: $*p < .05$, $***p < .001$.

Source: Graduation data; IPEDS 2004 collection year tracking fall 1998 graduation cohort; institutions; NSSE 2005 and 2004 institutions that fell into one of the five main Carnegie classifications and were able to report graduation information to IPEDS in 2004.

students who started college in 1998. The student engagement measures were collected in 2004 and 2005. Although institutional graduation rates do not change much from year to year, it is nonetheless the case that these graduation rate data and student engagement results represent different students.

At the same time, the magnitude of these correlations probably underestimates the strength of the relationships between student engagement and persistence. Because student engagement varies considerably within institutions, the relationships between NSSE benchmark scores and persistence may be even stronger for individual students. First- to second-year persistence data from Humboldt State (Hughes and Pace, 2003) also showed positive relationships between engagement and persistence.

Though smaller schools generally engage students more effectively, colleges and universities of similar sizes can vary widely. Figure 5—the EKG of student engagement—shows the senior academic challenge benchmark scores for the 600+ four-year schools that participated in the NSSE at least once between 2000 and 2003 (Kuh, 2003). Smaller schools are generally more academically challenging, in part because they have a lower student-faculty ratio, more

FIGURE 5
Level of Academic Challenge for Seniors, by Enrollment

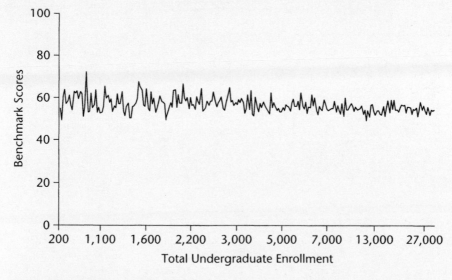

Source: National Survey of Student Engagement, 2005.

full-time faculty, and more classes with fewer than twenty students (National Survey of Student Engagement, 2005). At the same time, some large universities are more engaging than many smaller colleges. This pattern holds for the other clusters of effective educational practice. Similar patterns exist at two-year colleges, with some larger institutions being more engaging on average than small ones (K. McClenney, personal communication, March 9, 2006). So estimating institutional performance in terms of student engagement requires probing more deeply into the nature of the student experience at a particular institution because not all colleges of certain types and sizes are comparable on these types of indicators.

Student engagement varies more within *any given school or institutional type than* between *schools or institutional types.* This statement may sound counterintuitive, but it is consistent with other research (Pascarella and Terenzini, 2005). To illustrate, Figure 6 shows the range of student-faculty interaction benchmark scores of first-year students at twelve different baccalaureate liberal

FIGURE 6
Student-Faculty Interaction for First-Year Students at Twelve Liberal Arts Colleges

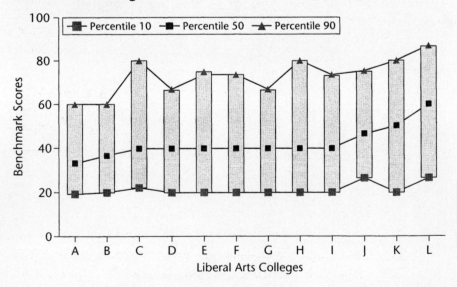

Source: National Survey of Student Engagement, 2005.

arts colleges, ranging from the lowest-scoring school on this benchmark to the highest scoring (Kuh, 2003). At this type of institution, we might expect student contact with faculty to be relatively high across the board. The figure shows only the middle 80 percent of students at each institution so that outliers do not skew the display. Note that the distance between the mean scores of the lowest- (31) and highest-scoring (59) schools is quite substantial, about 28 points, or more than one quarter of the 100-point scale, suggesting that instead of a fairly uniform pattern of high student-faculty interaction at small liberal arts colleges, there are instead very large differences in this sector. Equally important, the pattern represented in Figure 6 is similar for the other NSSE benchmarks of effective educational practice for all other types of four-year colleges and universities, indicating that student engagement varies more *within* institutions and categories of institutions than it does *between* schools or types of schools.

Student engagement in effective educational practice is unrelated to selectivity (Kuh and Pascarella, 2004; National Survey of Student Engagement, 2003). The combined SAT or ACT scores of entering students are independent of student participation in educationally purposeful activities. That is, although highly selective institutions can claim that their students are likely to benefit from being around highly able peers, no evidence exists, for example, that students attending these colleges and universities interact more with faculty members, have more experiences with diversity, or participate more frequently in active and collaborative learning activities (Kuh and Pascarella, 2004; Pascarella and others, 2005).

Some groups of students are typically somewhat more engaged than others. Exhibit 2 lists the groups of students that are *on average* more engaged than others. Full-time students and students who live on campus (the vast majority of whom are enrolled full time) are more engaged. It is to be expected, as they take more classes per academic term, read and write more, and spend more time preparing for class than their part-time counterparts. Because they live on campus, they have easier access than their commuting peers to faculty members, other students, and other institutional resources. In addition, full-time students tend to have fewer obligations such as family responsibilities and off-campus work that might preclude them from taking part in certain educational activities (study abroad or extracurricular events, for example) (Kuh, 2003). As we

EXHIBIT 2
Who's More Engaged?

- Women
- Full-time students
- Students living on campus
- Students who start at and graduate from the same school
- Learning community students
- International students
- Students with diversity experiences

illustrate later, full-time students also have more experiences with diversity such as having serious conversations with peers from different racial or ethnic backgrounds or who hold different political or social views.

Some single-mission institutions confer engagement advantages to their students. In general, for example, women at single-sex colleges are more engaged than women at private coeducational institutions (Kinzie, and others, 2007). That is, both first-year and senior women attending women's colleges report:

- Higher levels of academic challenge,
- More active and collaborative learning,
- More interaction with faculty members, and
- More diversity-related experiences.

Graduates of women's colleges have higher educational and career aspirations than their counterparts at coed institutions (Pascarella and Terenzini, 2005). The perceptions of the campus environment on women's college campuses are somewhat mixed, however, in that seniors at women's colleges perceived a lower level of interpersonal support, while first-year students at women's colleges perceived greater support for success.

Finally, NSSE data indicate that, compared with women at coed institutions, women at single-sex colleges report:

- Greater gains in understanding themselves and others,
- Greater gains in general education, and
- Greater gains in their ability to analyze quantitative problems.

Bridges, Kinzie, Nelson Laird, and Kuh (forthcoming) examined the nature of student engagement at minority-serving institutions (MSIs) and predominantly white institutions (PWIs), analyzing records from about sixteen thousand Hispanic and Latino students from thirty-six Hispanic-serving institutions (HSIs) (twenty-six public, ten private) and 639 PWIs (274 public, 365 private) as well as twenty-three thousand African American students from thirty-seven historically black colleges and universities (HBCUs) (23 public, 14 private) and 650 PWIs (276 public, 374 private). On balance, it appears that cultural capital plays a role in the type of institution a student chooses to attend, but the dynamic differs for African Americans and Hispanics, depending on the type of institution they attend. For example, although differences in student engagement for Hispanic students at HSIs and PWIs are generally quite small (effect sizes between −0.20 and 0.20), attending an HSI appears to have a compensatory effect. That is, without statistical controls for student background characteristics, the effects of Hispanic students attending HSIs tend to be unfavorable. When controls for gender, mother's education, enrollment status, and transfer status are entered, however, the results for HSIs improve slightly. In fact, controlling for student characteristics when they enter college, HSIs show a few, albeit very small, positive effects. Seniors benefit the most from active and collaborative learning and show greater gains in understanding people of other races and ethnicities (Bridges, Kinzie, Nelson Laird, and Kuh, forthcoming).

At HSIs where Hispanics made up 10 percent or more of the faculty, however, students interacted more often with faculty and participated more frequently in active and collaborative learning activities and enriching educational experiences such as community service (Bridges, Kinzie, Nelson Laird, and Kuh, forthcoming). This finding is consistent with other research showing that minority faculty members across all institutional types are more likely to use effective educational practices, compared with white faculty members (Kuh, Nelson Laird, and Umbach, 2004).

The single best predictor of student satisfaction with college is the degree to which students perceive the college environment to be supportive of their academic and social needs. Perceptions of the college environment seem to matter to various forms of student engagement and other dimensions of student success, at least indirectly (Astin, 1993b; Pascarella and Terenzini, 2005). How students feel about their school does not necessarily directly affect how much they learn. But perceptions do directly affect student satisfaction and how much effort students will expend on educationally purposeful activities, which consequently have direct effects on their learning and personal development (Hu and Kuh, 2002, 2003b; Kuh, 2000; Kuh and Hu, 2001a, 2001b). Unfortunately, African Americans and Asian Americans are the least satisfied with their college experiences (National Survey of Student Engagement, 2005).

A Closer Look at Engagement in Effective Educational Practices

Evidence is mounting that participation in certain kinds of educational activities positively affect student learning and personal development (Association of American Colleges and Universities, 2007; Pascarella and Terenzini, 2005). This section summarizes some of the more important of these experiences.

Faculty-Student Contact

As mentioned earlier, numerous studies and reports point to the salutary effects associated with student contact with faculty members (Astin, 1977, 1985b, 1993b; Bean, 1985; Bean and Kuh, 1984; Education Commission of the States, 1995; Ewell, 1989; Feldman and Newcomb, 1969; Kuh and others, 1991; Lamport, 1993; Pascarella, 1985; Pascarella and Terenzini, 1976, 1979b, 1991, 2005; Terenzini, Pascarella, and Blimling, 1996; Terenzini, Springer, Pascarella, and Nora, 1995; Tinto, 1993). Informal student-faculty interaction activities—being a guest in a professor's home, working on a research project with a faculty member, talking with instructors outside of class, and serving on committees with faculty—are positively correlated with student learning and development (Astin, 1993b; Kuh, 2003; Kuh and Hu, 2001a).

Intentional programs to facilitate student-faculty interaction have different effects on students. For example, relationships with faculty predicted development of academic competence among new students in the first year of college (Reason, Terenzini, and Domingo, 2005), and sophomore success (in terms of GPA and satisfaction) was related to high-quality student-faculty interaction (Graunke and Woosley, 2005; Juillerat, 2000).

First-generation students who reported positive interactions with faculty and other college personnel were more likely to experience academic success (satisfactory GPA and persistence) and were more satisfied with their academic experience (Amelink, 2005). Whether these relationships are causal, however, is not known. That is, perhaps more satisfied students are more confident in seeking out faculty members rather than becoming more satisfied because of such contacts. In fact, Kuh and Hu (2001a) found that the effects of student-faculty interaction are conditional, with academically better prepared students who devoted more effort to their studies interacting more frequently with faculty members. It is not clear whether this outcome is because such students were more assertive in seeking out faculty members or whether faculty members encouraged students who performed well academically to make contact (such as writing laudatory comments in the margins of a student's paper, suggesting they talk further about the topic). Most likely, both forms of student and faculty behavior are operating (Bean and Kuh, 1984).

Mentoring activities, including faculty interaction outside class and contact with advisors, are positively related to African American student persistence at PWIs and HBCUs (Himelhoch, Nichols, Ball, and Black, 1997). Fries-Britt and Turner (2002) found that students at HBCUs attributed their success to the encouragement and support they received from faculty and staff. Similarly, strong relationships with faculty and staff appear to contribute to Latino students' sense of belonging and their feeling that they are valued and "matter" in the community (Dayton, Gonzalez-Vasquez, Martinez, and Plum, 2004). Likewise, among the distinctive strengths attributed to tribal colleges are high-quality student-faculty interactions that provide students personal attention and opportunities to integrate traditional values into the learning environment (American Indian Higher Education Consortium, Institute for Higher Education Policy, and Sallie Mae Education Institute, 2000). In general, for most students most of the time, the more interaction with faculty the better. Both substantive and social out-of-class contacts with faculty members appear to positively influence (though indirectly) what students get from their college experience, their views of the college environment (especially the quality of personal relations), and their satisfaction. The possible exceptions are meeting with faculty members about improving their written work and interacting with faculty informally outside the classroom (Kuh and Hu, 2001a). The former appears to be important to the development of academic skills and many desirable gains, but it also has a mild dampening effect on student satisfaction. It is possible that many students—especially in the first year—interpret faculty feedback on their writing to be overwhelmingly critical, while faculty members may intend to use criticism to challenge students to higher levels of performance. Good intentions notwithstanding, such feedback may come as a shock to many new students who earned relatively high grades in high school. At the same time, contact with faculty focused on writing improvement was positively related to the amount of time devoted to educationally purposeful college activities and gains.

Out-of-class contacts appear to positively shape students' perceptions of the campus environment and seem to positively influence educational aspirations (Gurin and Epps, 1975; Hearn, 1987; Pascarella, 1985) and degree completion (Pascarella, Smart, and Ethington, 1986; Stoecker, Pascarella, and Wolfe, 1988). Although the reason for this relationship is not clear, it seems likely that when faculty engage students outside the classroom and these interactions are positive, students may feel affirmed and develop a stronger bond with the institution (Kuh, Douglas, Lund, and Ramin-Gyurnek, 1994). These interactions may reinforce a student's initial goals and deepen the commitment to graduate (Pascarella and Terenzini, 1991, 2005). Primarily informal, social-oriented contacts, however, do not directly contribute to desired outcomes (Bean, 1980, 1985; Voorhees, 1987). In fact, some evidence suggests that students who have the most out-of-class contact with faculty report making less progress toward desired outcomes (Kuh and Hu, 2001a).

For some purposes, occasional contact with faculty members may be enough. To illustrate, three of the six behaviors on the NSSE student-faculty cluster are of this kind: discussing career plans, working with a faculty member outside class on a committee or project, and doing research with a faculty member. For most students, doing the first two once or maybe twice a semester is probably good enough. Working on a research project with a faculty member just once during college could be a life-altering experience. For other activities such as getting prompt feedback, discussing grades and assignments, and discussing ideas outside of class, the more frequent the contact the better (Kuh, 2004).

It is prudent to assume that technology will alter our understanding of the faculty role in the learning process. For example, after reviewing evidence from institutions participating in the Pew-funded Course Redesign Program conducted by the Center for Academic Transformation, Carol Twigg (2005) concluded that by using technology effectively, student success can be achieved in class without increased student-faculty contact. It requires being more intentional about the nature of the contact such as being available on an as-needed, "when students get stuck" basis, which is built into the redesign of mathematics courses at Virginia Tech, the University of Alabama, and the University of Idaho.

In the final analysis, student-faculty interaction is important because it encourages students to devote greater effort to other educationally purposeful activities. Both the *nature* and the *frequency* of the contacts matter (Kuh and Hu, 2001a; Pascarella and Terenzini, 2005). But the dynamics of how student contact with faculty contributes to this heightened and balanced engagement are not clear. Perhaps meeting and talking with faculty members empowers students to do more than they think they can and helps validate them as full members of the campus community, which in turn legitimates their presence and makes them more comfortable to reach out and become engaged in a variety of activities.

Peer Interactions

Whom students choose for friends and spend time with is important to what they do in college and how they feel about their experiences (Kuh, 1993). "A large part of the impact of college is determined by the extent and content of one's interactions with major agents of socialization on campus, namely, faculty members and student peers" (Pascarella and Terenzini, 1991, p. 620). In fact, according to Astin (1993b, p. 398), peers are "the single most potent source of influence," affecting virtually every aspect of development—cognitive, affective, psychological, and behavioral. Indeed, the differences in the experiences of students who commute to college and live in campus residences are likely to be indirect influences through the interactions that students have with faculty, staff, and peers.

Student interaction with peers can positively influence overall academic development, knowledge acquisition, analytical and problem-solving skills, and self-esteem (Kuh, 1993, 1995). Aleman (1994, p. 38) found that "for female friends in college, conversations with each other serve as vehicles to transgress the limits of dualistic thinking" or ways to go beyond the tendency of traditional-age students to think in either/or or black-and-white terms when dealing with complex issues. Female friendships may be models for peer-assisted learning, an "often neglected potent resource inherent in a student population" (Alexander, Gur, and Patterson, 1974, p. 175).

Certain peer interactions foster learning (Astin, 1993b, p. 385):

- Discussing course content with other students,
- Working on group projects for classes,
- Tutoring other students,
- Participating in intramural sports,
- Being a member of a social fraternity or sorority,
- Discussing racial or ethnic issues,
- Socializing with someone from a different racial or ethnic group,
- Being elected to a student office, and
- Spending time each week socializing or in student clubs or organizations.

Peer teaching and participation in peer tutorial programs also have a positive impact on learning and personal development for those who do the teaching (Goldschmid and Goldschmid, 1976), because students who teach other students must know the material more thoroughly than if they were only studying it for themselves (Annis, 1983; Bargh and Schul, 1980; Pace, 1990). Moreover, such students become more knowledgeable about the material to be taught, which is presumed to produce greater conceptual learning (Benware and Deci, 1984; Pascarella and Terenzini, 1991).

Peer interactions are particularly important with regard to social integration, because students are more likely to stay in school when they feel comfortable and connected to other students with similar interests and aspirations (Bean, 1980; Spady, 1970; Tinto, 1975, 1987). For this reason, perhaps, fraternity and sorority membership is positively related to persistence (Astin, 1975). In addition, institutions with higher levels of student social interaction also have higher levels of student educational aspirations (Pascarella, 1985). According to Pascarella and Terenzini (1991, p. 384), "Obtaining the bachelor's degree was positively influenced by attending a college with a high level of cohesion in the peer environment (the number of peers whom the student regarded as close friends) or where students frequently participated in college-sponsored activities and there was a high level of personal involvement with and concern for the individual student."

Experiences with Diversity

Peer interactions are a major contributor to experiences with diversity, which can have substantial and positive effects for virtually all students across a wide range of desirable college outcomes (Chang, 1999, 2000; Gurin, 1999; Hurtado, Milem, Clayton-Pedersen, and Allen, 1999; Orfield, 2001; Umbach and Kuh, 2006). Such experiences include:

- Attending an institution that encourages contact among students of different backgrounds,
- Talking with others of different races and ethnicities,
- Talking with others who are very different in terms of their religious beliefs or personal values, and
- Incorporating diverse perspectives into class discussions or written work.

First-year students were more likely than sophomores, juniors, and seniors to interact with students from different racial and ethnic backgrounds (Hu and Kuh, 2003a; National Survey of Student Engagement, 2005). These differences are likely a function of the fact that more first-year students live on campus close to people who are different.

Cocurricular Activities

Participation in cocurricular activities is positively related to persistence (Carroll, 1988; Christie and Dinham, 1991; Mallinckrodt, 1988; Mallinckrodt and Sedlacek, 1987; Nelson, Scott, and Bryan, 1984; Simpson, Baker, and Mellinger, 1980). Hanks and Eckland (1976) speculated that involvement in cocurricular activities may influence persistence in two ways: (1) students are connected psychologically and socially to an affinity group that is achievement oriented, which reinforces the desire to graduate, and (2) students engage in activities that help them develop skills and competencies that enable them to succeed in college (for example, interpersonal skills, self-confidence) (Pascarella and Terenzini, 2005).

The extent to which participation in cocurricular activities affects persistence seems to be conditional in that such participation influences students differently. Pascarella and Chapman (1983) and Pascarella and Terenzini (1979a) found that involvement had the greatest positive impact on persistence for students with lower levels of commitment to the institution and their educational goals; that is, the greater the commitment to attaining educational goals, the less important engagement in campus life is to persistence. Involvement has a greater positive effect on first-year persistence for women than for men (Ethington and Smart, 1986; Pascarella and Terenzini, 1983). Because a variety of out-of-class experiences seem to be related to student commitment to the institutions (for example, involvement in athletics, fraternity or sorority membership), participation in certain out-of-class activities and persistence through increased student commitment to the institution and to earning a degree seem to be linked.

Although involvement in cocurricular activities is positively associated with persistence and other desirable outcomes (Astin, 1977, 1993b; Kuh, 1993; Pascarella and Terenzini, 2005), more than two-fifths of students (43 percent first-year students, 48 percent seniors) at four-year colleges and 84 percent of students at two-year colleges spend *no time* on these activities (Community College Survey of Student Engagement, 2004; National Survey of Student Engagement, 2005).

Student Satisfaction

Student satisfaction with the institution is an important but sometimes overlooked variable in determining the quality of the undergraduate experience. Satisfaction represents a sense that the student feels he or she belongs at, and is loyal to, the institution (Lenning, Beal, and Sauer, 1980; Tinto, 1987) and is highly correlated with engagement (Astin, 1993b; Holland and Huba, 1991; National Survey of Student Engagement, 2005; Russel and Skinkle, 1990; Whitt, 1994), persistence (Pascarella and Terenzini, 1991; Tinto, 1987), and academic performance (Bean, 1980; Bean and Bradley, 1986; Bean and

Vesper, 1994; Pike, 1991, 1993). Student satisfaction seems to have a stronger effect on grades than vice versa (Bean and Bradley, 1986). Moreover, "the student's degree of satisfaction with the college experience proves to be much less dependent on entering characteristics ... and more susceptible to influence from the college environment" (Astin, 1993, p. 277).

Most students (86 to 87 percent) at two-year and four-year colleges judge the overall quality of their experience to be at least "good"; only 2 percent say it was "poor" (Community College Survey of Student Engagement, 2005; National Survey of Student Engagement, 2005). This finding applies to students at Tribal Colleges, where Boyer (1995) found that 88 percent of students were "satisfied" or "very satisfied" with their experience. Generally, the more interaction students have with their peers and with faculty, the more satisfied they are overall with the college experience (Astin, 1993b; Kuh, 2003; National Survey of Student Engagement, 2005).

Student Characteristics

Because the effects of college experiences on desired outcomes are conditional (Pascarella and Terenzini, 2005), it is instructive to briefly review the engagement patterns of different groups of students.

First-Generation Students

First-generation students tend to be less engaged than other students, perhaps in part because they have less tacit knowledge of and fewer experiences with college campuses and related activities, behaviors, and role models compared with second-generation college students (Pike and Kuh, 2005a). In addition, their parents are unable to help much, even if they are so inclined, as they too lack knowledge of, or in some instances may find off-putting, certain activities that could lead to greater levels of engagement (Kenny and Stryker, 1996; London, 1992). It is especially problematic for students attending institutions where the predominant racial, ethnic, or religious culture differs from their own and where they may encounter adjustment challenges (Allen, 1992).

Most studies of first-generation students tend to attribute their lower levels of academic and social engagement and learning and intellectual development to the immutable characteristic of being born to parents who did not go to college. Such findings may have been largely the result of the analytical approaches employed. Pike and Kuh (2005a) suggest that low levels of engagement are an *indirect* result of being the first in one's family to go to college and are more a function of lower educational aspirations and living off campus. Thus, those committed to improving success rates of first-generation students should address these proximate causes.

Race and Ethnicity

Some studies show that minority students must contend with circumstances that may prevent them from taking full advantage of learning opportunities, especially at PWIs (Crosson, 1988; Feagin, Vera, and Imani, 1996; Pierce, 1989; Turner, 1994). To some degree, it may be the result of cumulative disadvantages associated with substandard precollege educational preparation (Garcia, 2001; O'Brien and Zudak, 1998). A less-than-congenial postsecondary learning environment may also be a contributing factor (Allen, 1985).

NSSE and CCSSE studies show that in general students from different racial and ethnic backgrounds appear to engage in effective educational practices at comparable levels. But some exceptions are apparent:

Asian Pacific Americans and African Americans are somewhat more likely to take part in enriching educational experiences than their peers.

African Americans report more active and collaborative learning activities; Asian Pacific Americans are the least engaged in this area.

Latinos, Latinas, and whites are the groups most satisfied with their college experience; African American students are generally the least satisfied (National Survey of Student Engagement, 2005).

Black women attending community colleges tend to be more engaged than their male counterparts (Community College Survey of Student Engagement, 2005).

Relational mechanisms for coping with the stresses of college life may also vary between student groups (Hurtado, 1994; Hurtado, Carter, and Spuler, 1996). A study of Latino students (Hurtado and Carter, 1997) indicated the importance of belonging to campus religious and social-community organizations and discussing course topics with student peers outside class. Other research (Hernandez, 2000; Kenny and Perez, 1996) indicates the role that continuing relationships with off-campus family members play in the psychological well-being of racially and ethnically diverse first-year students.

International Students

Generally speaking, international students engage more often in effective educational practices than their American counterparts, especially in the first year. International students:

- Report greater academic challenge,
- Interact more with faculty members,
- Engage more in diversity-related activities,
- Perceive the campus environment to be more supportive, and
- Report greater gains in personal and social development, practical competence, and general education.

First-year international students report higher levels of active and collaborative learning than their American peers but spend significantly less time relaxing and socializing. By the senior year, international students are more like American students in terms of socializing (Zhao, Kuh, and Carini, 2005).

Transfer Students

NSSE data (2005) show that senior transfer students share many characteristics with older students and commuters but differ in marked ways from their counterparts who persist at the same college where they started. These patterns hold even after controlling for institutional characteristics (sector, size, Carnegie type) and student characteristics (sex, enrollment status, age, race). For example, transfer students from two-year institutions:

- Interacted less with faculty, and
- Participated in fewer educationally enriching activities.

Transfer students from four-year institutions:

- Did more active and collaborative learning,
- Participated in fewer educationally enriching activities,

- Viewed the campus as less supportive,
- Gained less during college, and
- Were less satisfied overall with college.

Compared with seniors who began and persisted at their current institution, students who transferred later in their course of studies reported that at the time of their initial enrollment at their current institution they:

- Interacted less with faculty,
- Participated in fewer educationally enriching activities, and
- Gained less from college than their peers.

Fraternity and Sorority Members

Students who belong to Greek-letter organizations are generally as or more engaged than other students in educationally effective practices (Hayek, Carini, O'Day, and Kuh, 2002). This participation includes the amount of effort they put forth inside and outside the classroom (including experiences and exposure to diversity), self-reported gains in various dimensions of educational and personal growth, and perceptions of the campus environment (see also Pike, 2003). These findings run counter in some ways to the research showing mixed or negative relationships between membership in Greek-letter organizations and desired student learning and personal development outcomes (Astin, 1993b; Blimling, 1989, 1993; Pascarella and others, 1996; Pascarella, Palmer, Moye, and Pierson, 2001; Pike and Askew, 1990).

The overall favorable Greek effect on engagement extends to all segments of Greek membership—men and women, first-year and senior students, and to a lesser extent those who lived in the fraternity or sorority house or elsewhere, on or off campus. Though living in Greek housing did not negatively affect student engagement, the results do not necessarily refute the possibility that Greek housing might be linked to lower educational outcomes for some students (Blimling, 1989, 1993). Much of the commentary about the potential ill effects of living in Greek housing focuses on the well-being and educational experience of first-year students and newly initiated sophomores, not seniors. First-year students living in Greek housing spent more time in extracurricular activities with no appreciable diminution of time in other activities. Although participating in these activities may aid social integration and positively influence persistence, it also suggests that the time commitments of first-year Greek members may well be stretched beyond those of their nonmember counterparts, making it difficult to balance their studies with responsibilities to their new organization and activities for new members (Hayek, Carini, O'Day, and Kuh, 2002).

Student Athletes

On balance, it appears that student athletes, including those participating in high-profile sports (men's football and basketball, women's basketball), participate as often or more often as their nonathlete peers in effective educational practices (National Survey of Student Engagement, 2005; Umbach and Kuh, 2004; Umbach, Palmer, Kuh, and Hannah, 2004). These findings differ from those of recent highly publicized reports featuring athletes at highly selective four-year colleges (Bowen and Levin, 2003; Shulman and Bowen, 2001). For example, first-year high-profile student athletes show some signs of being less academically challenged than their lower-profile athletic peers. For example, both male Division II and female Division I high-profile athletes are less likely to spend sixteen or more hours a week preparing for class than their lower profile peers. In addition:

High-profile Division I senior female athletes see their campus environment as more supportive than other women athletes.

First-year women in Division III high-profile sports are slightly less engaged across the five NSSE measures of effective educational practices, compared with Division III women in lower-profile sports.

Compared with their nonathlete peers, high-profile student athletes are as engaged and often more engaged in effective educational practices:

Student athletes (both high-profile and other sports) at Division I institutions are more satisfied with the quality of their academic advising than are their nonathlete peers.

Compared with other seniors, student athletes are more likely to participate in community service projects, culminating senior experiences, and foreign language courses, regardless of gender or division of play.

Senior women at Division I institutions report participating in more enriching educational activities, see the campus as more supportive of their educational and social needs, and report gaining more in terms of speaking clearly and persuasively and understanding people from backgrounds different from their own (National Survey of Student Engagement, 2005).

Summary

The evidence from scores of studies over several decades strongly indicates that student engagement in effective educational practices seems to benefit all types of students to varying degrees.

Student engagement is related to a host of positive outcomes, including persistence, grades, and satisfaction.

Student-faculty interaction matters most to learning when it encourages students to devote greater effort to other educationally purposeful activities during college.

Student engagement varies more in institutions than between institutions.

Some students—such as first-generation students, males, transfer students, and those who live off campus—are generally less engaged than others.

Some emerging research suggests the engagement may have compensatory effects for at-risk students, including low-income and first-generation students and students of color attending PWIs. These findings suggest that seeking ways to channel student energy toward educationally effective activities would be wise, especially for those who start college with two or more risk factors. How institutions can do so is the subject of the next chapter.

Notes

1. The relationship between engagement and desired outcomes of college is well documented: Anaya, 1996; Astin, 1984, 1993b; Berger and Milem, 1999; Braxton, Sullivan, and Johnson, 1997; Carini, Kuh, and Klein, 2006; Chickering and Reisser, 1993; Goodsell, Maher, and Tinto, 1992; Hu and Kuh, 2003b; Hurtado and Carter, 1997; Jones and Watt, 1999; Kuh, 1995, 2001, 2003; Kuh and Hu, 2001b;

Kuh, Hu, and Vesper, 2000; Kuh, Kinzie, Schuh, Whitt, and Associates, 2005; Kuh and Pascarella, 2004; Kuh and others, 1991; Liddell and Davis, 1996; National Survey of Student Engagement, 2001, 2002, 2003, 2004, 2005; Pascarella and Terenzini, 1991, 2005; Pike, 1993; Pike and Kuh, 2005a; Stage, 1989; Stage and Hossler, 2000; Zhao and Kuh, 2004.

2. At two-year colleges, 58 percent of African American, Hispanic, and Native American students, compared with 72 percent of white students, reported overall grade averages of A or B (Community College Survey of Student Engagement, 2005). At four-year schools, white students reported the highest grades, Asian and multiracial students somewhat lower grades, Latina, Latino, and Native American students lower grades still, and African American students the lowest grades. For example, 52 percent of Latinos reported GPAs of 2.49 and below, compared with 68 percent of whites who earned GPAs of 2.50 and above (Swail with Redd and Perna, 2003).

Institutional Conditions Associated with Student Success

T HIS CHAPTER DISTILLS THE INSTITUTIONAL CONDITIONS and promising policies and practices that foster student success. What institutions can do in this regard is of particular interest, because they have some direct—if only modest—influence over these factors. Thus knowing the policies and practices and other institutional conditions related to student success and how to create them are vital to efforts to develop student-friendly campus cultures. Indeed, "if, as it appears, individual effort or engagement is one of the critical determinants of the impact of college, then it is important to focus on the ways in which an institution can shape its academic, interpersonal, and extracurricular offerings to encourage *student engagement*" (emphasis added) (Pascarella and Terenzini, 2005, p. 602).

Much of the pertinent literature is contained in national reports and studies such as "Seven Principles for Good Practices in Undergraduate Education" (Chickering and Gamson, 1987) and *Making Quality Count in Undergraduate Education* (Education Commission of the States, 1995), which summarizes the key concepts associated with student success and strong institutional performance. Carey (2004), Kuh, Kinzie, Schuh, Whitt, and Associates (2005), and Tagg (2003) describe programs and practices at educationally effective institutions. Other recent reports such as *The Road Less Traveled? Students Who Enroll in Multiple Institutions* (Peter and Cataldi, 2005) and *Community College Students: Goals, Academic Preparation, and Outcomes* (Hoachlander, Sikora, and Horn, 2003) are instructive for looking at programs and practices that work with different groups of students. Bailey and Alfonso (2005) and Bauman and others (2005) offer further evidence of how institutions can organize their resources and create success-oriented cultures. Also relevant is emerging research associated with the ongoing Building Engagement and Attainment of Minority Students project, the Making Excellence Inclusive initiative of the Association of American Colleges and Universities' (AAC&U), *Creating Role Models for Change: A Survey of Tribal College Graduates* (American Indian Higher Education Consortium, Institute for Higher Education Policy, and Sallie Mae Education Institute, 2000), the Diversity Scorecard (Bensimon, 2004), and the work of Hurtado, Dey, Gurin, and Gurin (2003) on the value of diversity and inclusion of underrepresented populations in higher education.

The institutional conditions shown in the lower right corner of Figure 7 include a sample of the programs and activities many colleges and universities offer. To examine the relationships between student success and institutional conditions, we summarize the literature across four broad, overlapping categories: structural and organizational characteristics, programs and practices, teaching and learning approaches, and student-centered campus cultures. The effects on student performance, however, are greater than the sum of these conditions in that they work together in an inclusive, mutually shaping, holistic way

FIGURE 7
The Relationship Between Student Success and Institutional Conditions

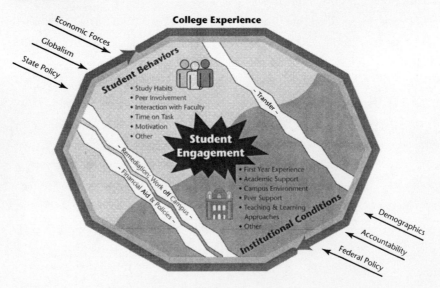

to enhance student and institutional performance. Equally important, to the extent institutions intentionally organize their resources to induce higher levels of student engagement, they may be adding value to the student experience.

Structural and Organizational Characteristics

Structural characteristics of institutions include such features as size, sector, control, mission, residential character, student-faculty ratio, endowment, and structural diversity (defined as the percentages of students from different racial and ethnic backgrounds). In general, the effects of these sorts of institutional characteristics on most measures of student success are trivial or inconclusive when controlling for student characteristics (Pascarella and Terenzini, 2005). For four-year institutions, the effects of different institutional characteristics on student change are both small and inconsistent because of a variety of factors such as methodological problems, lack of accurate measures, and student-institution level of analysis complications that make it difficult to estimate the impact of structural conditions on student success. Nevertheless, some structural characteristics appear to be consistently related to traditional measures of student success. For example, because selectivity and persistence are highly correlated, it is expected that institutions enrolling academically well-prepared students will graduate them at higher rates (Saupe, Smith, and Xin, 1999).

Institutional Attribute: Size

Institutional size is inversely related to student persistence and degree completion, although as with other areas, its impact is small and indirect in that the mediating effect is transmitted through other intervening variables (Pascarella and Terenzini, 2005). For example, size appears to shape students' enrollment decisions through students' perceptions of the institutional environment, faculty and peer interactions, and students' academic and social involvement. As noted previously, smaller four-year institutions are generally more engaging than larger institutions (National Survey of Student Engagement, 2002, 2003), in part because they have more favorable faculty-student ratios and more small classes, making it easier for faculty to know students by name, for students to know their peers, and for students to participate actively in classes. Further, many small colleges are geographically isolated, which increases the chances that students will live near one another and close to the campus and contributes to social and academic integration.

Testing Bean's student attrition model with institution-level constructs from Berger and Milem's college impact model (2000), Titus (2004) found that the only institution-level variables that influenced student persistence were size and selectivity. Titus concluded that differences between institutions may not be as important as differences between students in terms of their educational goals, college experiences, and institutional commitment. In other words, college student persistence is influenced by complex factors, most of which are student-level factors such as gender, socioeconomic status, enrollment patterns, and engagement levels.

Institutional Attribute: Sector

Although two- and four-year colleges differ with respect to such features as selectivity and residential living options, Pascarella, Bohr, Nora, and Terenzini (1995) found few significant differences between two- and four-year college samples in their examination of first-year gains made on four cognitive measures—reading comprehension, mathematics, critical thinking, or a composite measure of all three tests. The two-year sector had slightly higher end-of-first-year scores in mathematics, while students at the four-year institutions had slight advantages in reading comprehension and critical thinking. Women derived slightly greater cognitive benefits from four-year institutions than men, while men gained more than women at two-year institutions. Nonwhite students gained more at two-year institutions, while white students gained more at four-year institutions. These findings suggest that differences in institutional resources, library size, faculty-student ratio, and campus physical and recreation facilities probably have trivial influences on cognitive and intellectual gains.

Institutional resources and reputation featured in college rankings are largely irrelevant to high-quality educational experiences as measured by student engagement in educationally purposeful activities (Kuh and Pascarella, 2004; Pike, 2004). Recall, too, that institutional selectivity has little impact on measures of student learning, particularly critical thinking (Pascarella, 2001; Pascarella and others, 2005). This research suggests that enrollment management activities, guidebooks, and efforts to help students make choices on these characteristics overemphasize the importance of these institutional characteristics to student learning. Instead, what matters to developmentally powerful undergraduate learning experiences is the vitality of classroom experiences combined with students' own effort and study habits (Astin, 1993b; Kuh, 2003; Kuh, Kinzie, Schuh, Whitt, and Associates, 2005; Kuh and Pascarella, 2004; Volkwein and others, 2000).

Structural Diversity

Structural diversity of a campus positively affects student outcomes (American Council on Education and American Association of University Professors, 2000; Hurtado, Milem, Clayton-Pedersen, and Allen, 1998). A more diverse student body is associated with greater interaction among the groups and more positive relations among students (Hurtado, Dey, Gurin, and Gurin, 2003; Pascarella, 2001), in part because it increases the probability that students will interact with peers from different backgrounds (Gurin, 1999). Such interactions positively affect critical thinking (Pascarella, Palmer, Moye, and Pierson, 2001) and make students more susceptible to subsequent diversity experiences (Pascarella and others, 1996; Whitt and others, 2001). Students who have more frequent experiences with diversity also report:

- More progress in personal and educational growth,
- More involvement in active and collaborative learning, and
- Higher levels of satisfaction with their college experience.

Diversity experiences also vary by institutional type. Students at doctoral/research-extensive universities are slightly more likely than their counterparts attending other types of four-year institutions to interact with students from different backgrounds, perhaps because there are proportionately more students from diverse backgrounds attending such institutions (Hu and Kuh, 2003a). It might also be a result of concerted efforts to provide diversity-related programming (Kuh and Umbach, 2005; Pike and Kuh, 2006). Umbach and Kuh (2006) reported that students at liberal arts colleges are the most likely to engage in diversity-related activities, while students at master's institutions are the least likely. Pike, Smart, Kuh, and Hayek (2006) found that attending a doctoral/research university or a master's university as opposed to a baccalaureate general college was not significantly related to informal interactional diversity. Likewise, neither location in an urban area nor size (full-time equivalent enrollment) was related to informal interactional diversity. Density of racial and ethnic groups is important as students are somewhat more likely to engage in diversity-related activities on campuses with larger proportions of students of color, regardless of institutional type.

Consistent with Kuh and Umbach's findings (2005), HBCU students report fewer experiences with diversity, compared with students elsewhere. This outcome is to be expected, given that HBCU enrollments are slightly more than 80 percent African American on average (Provasnik and Shafer, 2004). Contrary to some other research, Bridges, Kinzie, Nelson Laird, and Kuh (forthcoming) found that African American students at PWIs were more satisfied with their overall experience than African American HBCU students. In addition, first-year students at HBCUs did not perceive their campus environment as supportive as their counterparts at PWIs, especially in terms of providing academic support. Informal interactional diversity was negatively related to being a public institution but positively related to being a liberal arts college. A substantial positive relationship existed between structural diversity and informal interactional diversity (Bridges, Kinzie, Nelson Laird, and Kuh, forthcoming).

In addition, diversity experiences also vary substantially by major field. Seniors majoring in math, science, and engineering disciplines have the fewest experiences with diversity; students in the social sciences and humanities report the most. More than half of social sciences and humanities majors said they frequently had serious conversations with students of a different race or ethnicity than their own, compared with only about a quarter (26 percent) of engineering majors and a third (36 percent) of physical science majors (National Survey of Student Engagement, 2004).

Organizational Structure

Using Birnbaum's conceptual framework (1988), Berger (2002) found that the organizational structure of an institution, defined as the patterns and processes of behaviors exhibited by administrators on campus, has some influence on student learning. Colleges that were more externally oriented and less focused on internal aspects of the campus had a negative relationship to student learning (represented by student self-ratings of academic ability, educational gains, and GPA); campuses with a collegial ethos also had some negative effects, suggesting that strong relationships among faculty and administrators may not directly affect student learning. Bureaucratic dimensions had no significant effect, while institutions featuring stories and myths to shape behavior and decision making (the symbolic dimension) had mixed effects on student learning outcomes. Godwin and Markham's case study (1996) of the effects of bureaucratic organizational structure on new student college adjustment and socialization at a large state university revealed that new students were frustrated by waiting in lines, "getting the runaround," and excessive paperwork. As a result, new students developed coping mechanisms ranging from accepting such bureaucratic dysfunctions as the natural order and conforming to confront inefficiencies. Although bureaucratic structures seem to have a trivial at best impact on student learning, they influence new students' socialization. Given Braxton and McClendon's finding (2001–02) that effective communication of rules and regulations positively affects students' integration and persistence, how new students perceive and interact with the bureaucratic elements of the institution may well affect their success.

Institutional Mission

Organizational theory suggests that institutional mission, which is generally denoted by sector difference or institutional type, is related to student success because colleges and universities that align their mission with their educational policies and programs generally are more effective and efficient (Birnbaum, 1991; Bolman and Deal, 1991; Ewell, 1989). According to Chickering and Reisser (1993, p. 287), "Clear and consistent objectives, stated in terms of desired outcomes for learning and personal development, are critically important in creating an educationally powerful institution. [They] should not have to be deduced from course descriptions. They should be explicit and compelling. They should be defined by the members of the college community, taken to heart by campus leaders, and invoked as guides to decision-making."

For example, the extent to which a campus has an enacted mission that makes an explicit commitment to the success of all students appears to be related to graduation rates, persistence, and student engagement (Kezar and Kinzie, 2006; Kuh, Kinzie, Schuh, Whitt, and Associates, 2005). Ewell (1989) found that the match between actual program delivery and intended purpose and the degree to which people on campus agree on the mission are important to students' academic development. These studies suggest that the espoused, written institutional mission appears to be less important than the enacted mission of a campus.

Small liberal arts colleges are generally associated with greater gains in terms of student engagement and general education outcomes (Hu and Kuh, 2002; Kuh and Siegel, 2000; Pascarella, Pierson, Wolniak, and Terenzini, 2004). Although Carnegie type was related to certain areas of student engagement, it is probable that other institutional characteristics have a greater influence on it (Pike and Kuh, 2005b). In fact, after taking into account the background characteristics of students, differences by institutional type tend to diminish (Pike, Kuh, and Gonyea, 2003). In addition, Kuh, Kinzie, Schuh, Whitt, and Associates (2005) found that institutions with higher-than-predicted graduation rates and levels of student engagement differed considerably in terms of Carnegie classification type, control, and selectivity yet had policies and practices in place that appeared to engage students at high levels. Elements of the institutional culture and the complementary practices employed appeared to explain more of what mattered to student success than the types of institutional or student characteristics typically examined in research. This finding is consistent with Blose's observation (1999) that because the biggest differences between institutions in terms of persistence and graduation rates is the amount of time it takes to earn a degree, low graduation rates may be partly a function of institutional conditions that impede academic progress, including course availability and scheduling and problems with advising.

Transfer rates are a legitimate indicator of student success, particularly in the two-year sector (Dougherty, 1994; London and Shaw, 1996; Nora, 1999; Rendon and Garza, 1996; Rifkin, 1998; Rosenbaum, 1998). The transfer mission is particularly important to the educational attainment and success of students from underserved populations, as two-year colleges serve as the gateway to the bachelor's degree for the majority of these students (National Articulation and Transfer Network, 2002; Rendon and Garza, 1996; Suarez, 2003). Strong transfer rates appear to be associated with clear articulation agreements between community colleges and four-year institutions (Nora, 1999; Rendon and Garza, 1996) and a deep institutional commitment to the transfer mission, where transfer to a four-year institution is a high priority and a shared responsibility of administrators, faculty, and counselors (Shaw and London, 2001; Suarez, 2003; Townsend, 1995). Access to accurate transfer procedures and financial aid information, counseling services, workshops on the transfer process, and orientation programs seem to help with transfer students' persistence and satisfaction (Alpern, 2000), perhaps because they help to demystify the process (Berger and Malaney, 2003; Cohen and Brawer, 1987; Cuseo, 1998; Rifkin, 1998; Suarez, 2003; Turner, 1988).

The assigned role of community colleges in a state system seems to affect associate's degree completion rates and transfer rates. For example, if the community college is viewed as a transfer college for its state's university system, then transfer rates tend to be higher. If viewed as both a site for transfer and preparation for immediate employment, then transfer rates are usually lower. Moreover, variations in transfer rates can be predicted by whether a state's community colleges emphasize technical or comprehensive programs and which of these functions institutional policies support (Cohen, 1996).

Minority-Serving Institutions

Certain special mission institutions—HBCUs, HSIs, and tribal colleges— appear to benefit their students educationally and socially (Allen, 1992; Dayton, Gonzalez-Vasquez, Martinez, and Plum, 2004; Outcalt and Skewes-Cox, 2002). Strong support systems, which help create a success-oriented environment, explain in part HBCU students' better academic performance, higher graduation rates, and higher occupational aspirations, compared with those of their African American counterparts at PWIs (Allen, 1992; Astin, Tsui, and Avalos, 1996). For example, Terenzini and others (1997) found that first-year HBCU students received greater peer encouragement to remain enrolled than their counterparts attending PWIs, indicating the power of the peer group at HBCUs. Women's colleges also enjoy small to modest advantages in terms of persistence rates. Moreover, despite most being underresourced, HBCUs have developed programmatic interventions that seem to foster high expectations for intellectual development and academic support associated with cognitive gains for African American students similar to those found at PWIs (Kim, 2002; Pascarella, 2001).

At four-year institutions, African Americans attending HBCUs are more likely to complete their degree than their counterparts at PWIs. The magnitude of these positive effects vary, depending on the study. "Astin, Tsui, and Avalos (1996) found the advantage to be about 6 percentage points; Ehrenberg and Rothstein (1994) estimated the advantage to be between 9 and 29 percentage points, depending on the model used" (Pascarella and Terenzini, 2005, p. 394). Kim (2002) asserted that certain outcomes such as academic performance for African American students at HBCUs and PWIs are more a function of precollege differences in students' educational preparation than of institutional environments. The weight of the evidence suggests, however, that attending an HBCU has significant positive effects, especially for persistence and graduation rates.

Another distinction of HBCUs is that they serve as gateways to advanced degrees for African American students, similar to what many liberal arts colleges do for white students (Gumport, 2001). Attending an HBCU has a net positive effect on degree aspirations of African American students and their likelihood of enrolling in graduate school (Carter, 1999; Heath, 1992; Weiler, 1993) or entering a program in the sciences, engineering, or business (Redd, 2001; Wenglinsky, 1998), a major reason HBCUs are the primary producers of African American undergraduates who hold doctorates in science and engineering (Solorzano, 1995).

The small number of studies of Hispanic students at HSIs yields mixed results (Abraham, Lujan, Lopez, and Walker, 2002; Benitez, 1998; Dayton, Gonzalez-Vasquez, Martinez, and Plum, 2004; Laden, 1999, 2001, 2004). According to Laden (2004, p. 193), "Many HSIs offer a variety of academic and student support programs and holistic approaches that are specifically designed to raise Latino student aspirations and enhance their retention and completion rates."

Programs and Practices

One direct way colleges and universities can affect what students do is by intentionally designing programs and practices that channel student behavior into educationally purposeful activities. Although many institutions make similar kinds of programs available, they do not always reach the intended audiences or have the desired effect.

New Student Adjustment

Coherent first-year experience programs, which include precollege and ongoing orientation programs, first-year seminars, and other new student advising and study group experiences, appear to be linked to a variety of positive outcomes for first-year students (Muraskin and Wilner, 2004; Reason, Terenzini, and Domingo, 2005; Upcraft, Gardner, and Barefoot, 2005; Upcraft, Mullendore, Barefoot, and Fidler, 1993). For example, the Pell Institute (2004) found that institutions with high graduation rates had more programs that eased new students' entry and adjustment to college, including bridge programs, learning communities, study groups, block registration of students, and tutoring. In addition, creating clear pathways to show students what to expect and what success looks and feels like helps students bring meaning to their educational experiences and helps acculturate them to the institution (Kuh, Kinzie, Schuh, Whitt, and Associates, 2005).

Orientation. Forest (1985) controlled for entering students' academic ability and found that institutions that provided the most extensive orientation and advising programs had higher graduation rates. Other studies show similar results (Dunphy, Miller, Woodruff, and Nelson, 1987; Fidler and Hunter, 1989). Orientation may also have a positive effect on persistence through its influence on social integration and subsequent commitment to the institution.

The NSSE (2005) reported that most (87 percent) first-year students attended an institution-sponsored orientation program. Those who did:

- Participated in more educationally enriching activities,
- Perceived the campus environment to be more supportive,
- Reported greater developmental gains during their first year of college, and
- Were more satisfied with their overall college experience.

Orientation programs are intended to facilitate students' transition to college and provide information to help them manage the challenges they encounter making their way in a new environment. After taking into account students' educational aspirations, commitment to graduation, academic aptitude, and socioeconomic status, however, student participation in orientation may have only a trivial, statistically nonsignificant direct effect on persistence (Pascarella and Terenzini, 1991, 2005). Despite this qualification, direct effects on persistence were found to be associated with longer comprehensive orientation programs, while even short summer orientation programs exert an indirect influence on students' persistence.

First-Year Seminars. First-year seminars take a variety of different forms. Some are an orientation to college, others are discipline based and taught by faculty members, and still others are team taught and combine advising and orientation activities and substantive, discipline-based or interdisciplinary content (Upcraft, Gardner, and Barefoot, 2005). Such courses are relatively common. For example, the NSSE (2005) reported that more than half (54 percent) of all first-year students participated in a course specifically designed to enhance their academic skills or social development.

Pascarella and Terenzini (2005) found only one study using an experimental design (Strumpf and Hunt, 1993) that estimated the impact of a freshman-year seminar. New students at the University of Maryland, College Park, interested in taking the seminar were randomly assigned to two groups, one that took the freshman-year seminar and the other that did not. Two years later, those that completed the freshman-year seminar were more likely to have stayed in school.

The NSSE (2005) findings show additional benefits for students who participated in a first-year seminar. Controlling for a variety of student and institutional characteristics, findings show that those in a freshman-year seminar:

- Were more challenged academically,
- Reported more active and collaborative learning activities,
- Interacted more frequently with faculty,
- Perceived the campus environment as being more supportive,
- Gained more from their first year of college, and
- Made greater use of campus services.

Carstens (2000) found that students who completed a first-semester orientation course earned more credit hours per semester and expended greater effort toward academic tasks three years after enrollment than their peers in a matched sample who had not taken the course. After controlling for student characteristics, the least academically prepared students earned more credit hours per term, had higher grades, and reenrolled at significantly higher rates than did their peers who did not take the orientation course; even students with higher entering ability had more positive academic outcomes than their no-course counterparts (Carstens, 2000).

Early Warning Systems. Early warning systems are especially important for students who start college with two or more risk factors (see Exhibit 1) or who appear to be struggling academically. Midterm progress reports, course-embedded assessments, and early alert systems that incorporate a network of individuals (faculty, mentors, academic support units, peer support groups) are most effective at helping students address these early adjustment difficulties (Kuh, Kinzie, Schuh, Whitt, and Associates, 2005; Tagg, 2003). Student retention, progression to degree, and graduation at HBCUs are fostered when at-risk students are identified early and intervention strategies are employed (Nettles, Wagener, Millett, and Killenbeck, 1999). Specially designed academic support programs that provide early intervention to prepare and assist students from historically underrepresented groups and other institutionally designed initiatives typically include early warning systems to identify and support students at academic risk.

Advising

Structured academic advising is important for helping students find their way through college at both two- and four-year institutions (Cohen and Brawer, 1996; Kramer and Associates, 2003). Although advising takes many forms in postsecondary education and it is difficult to tease out the effects of, for example, advising delivered by professional advisors or faculty members, high-quality advising seems to be positively related to student success. That is, although studies that did not control for the perceived quality of advising found mixed results (Aitken, 1982; Brigman, Kuh, and

Stager, 1982; Kowalski, 1977), Tinto (2004) found that advising positively affects retention and graduation when advisors address the needs of undecided students, those who decide to change their major, and first-generation students, who may not have the same knowledge of how to successfully navigate higher education. Like orientation, the quality of academic advising may also have an indirect effect when factors such as high school grades, gender, and age are taken into account (Metzner, 1989).

Advising is thought to be most effective in terms of promoting student success when integrated into academic support services and when sensitive to developmental needs of diverse students (Kramer and Associates, 2003). Advisors are particularly important in helping students plan their educational program appropriately and addressing questions of coherence and sequencing of the educational program—increasingly important as more students attend multiple institutions for a college degree (McCormick, 2003).

The quality of academic advising also is the single most powerful predictor of satisfaction with the campus environment for students at four-year schools (National Survey of Student Engagement, 2005). Fortunately, most students are reasonably satisfied with the quality of their academic advising. Only 7 percent of first-year students describe it as "poor." At liberal arts colleges and general colleges, advising is "very good" for first-year students and even better for seniors. The NSSE data (2005) show that students who rate their advising as good or excellent:

- Are more likely to interact with faculty in various ways,
- Perceive the institution's environment to be more supportive overall,
- Are more satisfied with their overall college experience, and
- Gain more from college in most areas.

A smaller percentage (65 percent) of part-time first-year students say advising is good or excellent; more say advising is poor (11 percent). Perhaps the reason is that part-time students spend less time on campus and have less time to meet with an advisor, which may translate into less favorable ratings because students' needs are not being met. They are also twice as likely to be undecided in terms of major, which may require different types of advising skills, such as less information dispensing and more career exploration.

Campus Residences

Living on campus has long been associated with persistence and student success (Astin, 1993b; Chickering and Reisser, 1993). Students who live on campus generally interact more with faculty and peers and are more satisfied with their undergraduate experience (Pascarella and Terenzini, 1991, 2005). Consistent with the findings of Chickering and others (see Blimling, 1993), living on campus had a direct, positive effect on learning outcomes and the greatest total effect (combination of direct and indirect effects) on learning outcomes of any institutional characteristic. Living-learning centers and residentially based freshman interest groups have even stronger effects on average than living on campus.

That campus residence is relatively powerful is understandable because of the "propinquity principle" (Newcomb, 1966): living on campus puts students in close physical proximity so they cannot avoid being confronted on an almost daily basis by others who have views and backgrounds different from their own. Living on campus helps students develop social connections with peers who are dealing with similar challenges and difficulties. Social network theory (see "Major Theoretical Perspectives on Student Success in College") may in part explain why students who do not have an affinity group have more trouble persisting in college when they encounter difficulty.

The effects of living on campus are probably more indirect than direct in terms of persistence and degree completion (Pascarella and Terenzini, 2005), because students who live on campus have more opportunities to interact with peers and faculty members. They are also more positive about the campus social and intellectual climates and report greater personal growth and development.

Learning Communities

Learning communities, programs that enroll groups of students in a common set of courses usually organized around a theme and frequently linked with residence life experiences, continue to be adopted at all types of colleges and universities as promising approaches to enrich student learning and student success (Knight, 2003; Shapiro and Levine, 1999; Tinto, 1997a, 1997b). The National Learning Communities Project monograph, *Learning Community*

Research and Assessment: What We Know Now (Taylor with Moore, MacGregor, and Lindblad, 2003), provides a comprehensive account of empirical evidence on learning communities and concludes that participation in a learning community was associated with student retention, student academic performance (GPA), credit hours earned, and student satisfaction. These findings hold for a variety of learning community settings and structures and types of students. Further evidence of the theoretical connections between learning communities and student engagement, self-reported gains in learning, and persistence have been fairly well documented (Knight, 2003; Pike, 1999; Pike, Schroeder, and Berry, 1997; Price, 2005; Zhao and Kuh, 2004).

Nationally, 29 percent of first-year students and 22 percent of seniors report participating (or planning to participate) in some type of learning community, defined as an experience where students take two or more of the same courses together (Zhao and Kuh, 2004). Learning communities are strongly related to all five of the NSSE clusters or benchmarks of effective educational practice, including diversity experiences, student self-reported gains in personal and social development, practical competence, general education, and overall satisfaction with the undergraduate college experience. Though positive for both first-year and senior students, the effects are greater for first-year students (as would be expected because they are more likely to have had the experience recently).

Figure 8 shows that first-year students at doctoral extensive and master's institutions have the highest learning community participation rates (about 30 percent). Certain students are most likely to gravitate to learning communities:

- Women,
- Full-time students,
- Students living in Greek housing,
- Nontransfer students,
- International students, and
- Students majoring in health-related fields; education; ethnic, cultural, and area studies; park, recreation, and sports management; agriculture; and liberal/general studies.

FIGURE 8
Learning Community Participation Rates, by Carnegie Classification

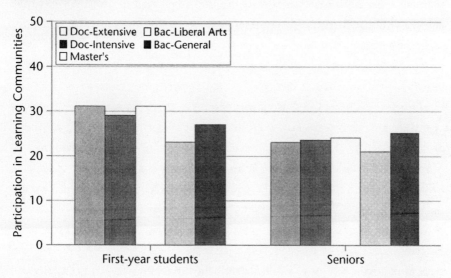

Participation in learning communities at the University of Texas at El Paso (UTEP) (2003) was related to increased first- to second-year persistence for students in science, technology, engineering, and mathematics. The UTEP learning community featured an orientation program, clustered discipline-based courses, and academic advising. Students in a similar program for women in science and engineering that added a residential component were more likely than their counterparts to persist; they also had higher grades and were more satisfied (Allen, Brower, and Golde, 1999). At Western Washington University (1996), participation in a two-year, cohort learning community designed for underrepresented minority students in law had a positive impact in terms of helping them make progress toward degree, enriching their learning, and facilitating their acceptance to law school.

The benefits of residential living-learning communities are fairly well documented (Taylor with Moore, MacGregor, and Lindblad, 2003). In their study of students in freshman interest groups, Pike, Schroeder, and Berry (1997) found that although residential learning communities did not improve students' academic achievement and persistence directly, they did indirectly improve students' success by enhancing their incorporation into college.

Participation in a freshman interest group was also associated with higher levels of involvement in campus activities, greater interaction with faculty outside the class and with peers, and higher levels of integration of course information (Schroeder, Minor, and Tarkow, 1999). This research corroborates the evidence that educational interventions in residence halls can have a positive effect on the quality of students' interaction with peers and faculty, which in turn enhances achievement and persistence.

Learning communities also appear to enhance the chances for success of commuter students attending community colleges (Tinto, 1997a; Tinto and Love, 1995). The Opening Doors Demonstration project (Bloom and Sommo, 2005) used a random assignment research design to study the effects of learning communities (three linked courses scheduled as a block with faculty integrating activities across courses) on student persistence and achievement. Students in the learning communities outperformed (higher pass rate in English) students not in a learning community. The effects of the program were even stronger in cases when faculty coordinated writing assignments and when students were aware that their instructors were working together. These studies are particularly noteworthy because they demonstrate the impact of learning communities on success among women, students of color, and other students in fields where they have been historically underrepresented.

Student Success Initiatives

Student success courses typically address issues such as optimal use of campus support resources and time management, advising and career development, and skill development such as goal setting and test and note taking (Gardner and Jewler, 1995). These courses have been credited with helping students learn effective study skills and improve retention of course material (Coleman and Freeman, 1996; Helmcamp and Petrie, 1998). The adaptive skills fostered in such courses are prerequisite behaviors that have direct and indirect influences on persistence and graduation. Furthermore, when academic support services are designed to meet student learning needs for particular courses, departments, or majors such as supplemental instruction or study groups linked to gateway courses, student persistence is enhanced (Tinto, 2004). Student success courses also support underrepresented students' adjustment to college. For example, participating in academic support courses and programs was found to contribute to a stronger sense of belonging among Latinos in college (Hurtado and Ponjuan, 2005). Linking academic support to the classroom is especially valuable to commuting students, who may have limited time on campus, and in ensuring that all students have access to academic support services.

When starting college, the vast majority of students (87 percent) say they will at least "occasionally" use campus academic support services such as writing skills centers. Yet by the end of the first year almost half (46 percent) had *not* done so. In contrast, only 15 percent *never* used campus recreational facilities. Between 40 and 50 percent of first-year students *never* used career planning, financial advising, or academic tutoring services. An Indiana University Bloomington study (Hossler, Kuh, and Olsen, 2001) showed that students in high-risk courses were almost twice as likely to seek tutoring when it was available in their own residence hall than when the same service was provided in other campus locations. Student use of academic skills centers jumped when the centers were moved closer to where students lived, thereby increasing access. Three such centers now operate in residence halls in different parts of the campus. Students who use these skill centers for mathematics and writing improvement are much more likely to persist to the second year and get higher grades than peers who do not, even though they are similar in most background characteristics, including academic ability (Hossler, Kuh, and Olsen, 2001). Thus simply providing services will not have the desired effect; students must be induced to use them.

About one-third of entering college students take developmental courses to bring their academic skills up to a level that will allow them to perform adequately in college (Bettinger and Long, 2005). Even so, debate continues about whether to limit the number of development courses a student can take, how much they cost (and thus divert funds from the core academic program), whether participants should receive academic credit, and whether the courses count toward graduation requirements. The research about the effects of such courses in community colleges—which deliver a disproportionate share of developmental courses nationally—is somewhat mixed. One study showed that taking remedial courses is associated with student retention (Hoyt, 1999).

Another (Bettinger and Long, 2005) indicated that students who take remediation courses were more likely to persist in college, compared with students with similar test scores and backgrounds who were not required to take the courses, and that participants were more likely to transfer to a higher-level college and to complete a bachelor's degree. In addition, developmental education courses were also found to play an important role in student success at institutions with high graduation rates (Pell Institute, 2004). At least one study produced contradictory findings (Burley, Cejda, and Butner, 2001). Remediation in English was found to have a positive effect on Latino students, which may help them overcome challenges associated with English being their second language (Swail, Cabrera, Lee, and Williams, 2005). Perhaps remediation helps students bring their performance up to levels that allow them to stay in school academically, even though their grades may not be comparable with those who do not require remediation.

By tailoring remediation programs to the specific characteristics of students needing such assistance, institutions are better able to serve and move students from developmental courses to college-level courses. The use of different methodologies and teaching strategies such as using intensive review formats or "refresher workshops" in math or grammar fundamentals to prepare returning adult students to take assessment and placement tests has been found to be a more efficient approach to moving returning adults into college-level courses (Ignash, 1997). In contrast, to address the needs of younger students, it is especially helpful when community colleges cooperate with high schools to clarify what college readiness means in terms of academic expectations and requirements and collaborate with schools to develop programs to meet high school students' developmental needs (Ignash, 1997; Rosenbaum, 1998). Despite some promising findings, more remains to be learned about the most effective approaches to working with students with weak academic skills at community colleges (Bailey and Alfonso, 2005; Boyland, 2002; Grubb, 2001). Exhibit 3 lists desirable characteristics of effective developmental education programs.

Student Support Services

Some evidence suggests that the ratio of student development professionals to students influences persistence. Hedlund and Jones (1970) found that all the

EXHIBIT 3
Recommended Components of Developmental Education Initiatives

- Required entry-level testing
- Mandatory placement in basic skills courses
- Required orientation programs
- No late registration options
- Dual enrollment in basic and college-level courses
- Reduced academic load for working students
- Comprehensive financial aid
- Incorporation of problem-solving skills in all developmental courses
- Limited number of courses allowed for remediation
- Continuous program evaluation
- Articulation between basic skills and college-level courses
- Institutionalization of precollege activities
- Developmental sequence of courses
- Early completion of sequence
- Course load restrictions even after completing sequence
- Early warning and academic progress information systems
- Continuous midterm program report
- Degree audit system for advising and frequent discussions about major and program intent
- Full-time director to organize and coordinate developmental education initiative

Sources: Ignash, 1997; Lucy-Allen, Merisotis, and Redmond, 2002.

two-year colleges in their sample with no greater than a 1:150 student development professional-to-student ratio graduated 50 percent or more of their students in two years, compared with the 20 percent graduation rate of the colleges with a ratio of more than 1:150. Astin (1993b) reported a similar relationship between persistence and resources allocated to student services and personnel. Pascarella and Terenzini (1991) cautioned, however, that such findings are confounded by many factors, including systematic differences in the ability of students attending certain institutions and the institution's enacted mission and ethos (Kuh, 1995). For example, perhaps institutions that invest in more student development professionals also have other attributes that promote student success that previous studies have not measured (Kuh, Kinzie, Schuh, Whitt, and Associates, 2005).

Lewis and Middleton (2003) emphasized the importance of a child-care facility on campus to African American persistence, transfer from two- to four-year institutions, and degree completion. Child care is also a major challenge facing low-income adults pursuing postsecondary education. Kappner (2002) found that when child care is provided on campus at the State University of New York, student parents are more likely to remain in school, graduate in fewer years, and earn higher grades. Other important services for adult learners are quiet work and study areas, academic support services available for extended hours, and family-oriented activities (Cook and King, 2005). Notably, the private, for-profit sector of postsecondary education seems to be more responsive in providing such services for adults than other sectors of higher education. Bailey, Badway, and Gumport (2001) found that student services such as admissions, counseling, and career placement were more integrated and better developed at the for-profit institutions than at the comparison community colleges in their study.

Teaching and Learning Approaches

Widespread use of effective pedagogical practices must be at the core of any agenda to promote student success. This area of research received more attention than any other over the past dozen years (Pascarella and Terenzini, 2005), fueled by the expanding research and theory on human learning (National Research Council, 2000). Widely disseminated papers (Barr and Tagg, 1995; Chickering and Gamson, 1987, 1991; Cross, 1998, 1999; Guskin, 1994, 1997; Hutchings, 1996) describe the value of restructuring the teaching and learning environment to shift the emphasis from faculty teaching to student learning (Barr and Tagg, 1995). This shift promises to have profound implications for setting higher expectations for students, for raising academic standards, for asking students to take more responsibility for their learning, for demonstrating competency through assessment, and for emphasizing and validating alternative ways of knowing, interdisciplinary methods, and problem-focused learning.

Educational Philosophy. "Faculty who show regard for their students' unique interests and talents are likely to facilitate student growth and development in every sphere—academic, social, personal, and vocational"

(Sorcinelli, 1991, p. 21). Maintaining an unshakable focus on student success is demonstrated in part by holding high expectations for all students and is a central feature of institutions with a student success–oriented educational philosophy. A key element of this approach is adhering to a talent development philosophy throughout the institution. In addition to recognizing that every student can learn under the right conditions, the talent development view requires that the institution organize its resources and create conditions for teaching and learning based on educationally effective practices.

The talent development view also recognizes the need to embrace and address students' diverse talents and needs (Chickering, 2006; Chickering and Gamson, 1987). Although appropriate for all students, this approach is particularly effective for working with students historically underserved in higher education, especially when pedagogical practices acknowledge and honor the life experiences of adult learners and view the talents and skills students bring to the classroom as "assets" rather than deficiencies. Such a view holds that because each student has a distinctive perspective on the world and the topic under study, all students enrich the learning of others as well as their own through sharing their knowledge and experience (Alexander and Murphy, 1994). Because faculty members often misunderstand, ignore, or devalue the talents of students from diverse backgrounds, these differences in learning style are sometimes viewed as academic deficiencies requiring remediation (Pounds, 1987). Treisman (1992) noted that many students from historically underserved groups at the University of California, Berkeley, were failing calculus, even though they had the academic prerequisites and demonstrated ability to perform successfully. He discovered that environmental disorientation was the problem, not lack of motivation as their instructors initially assumed. Treisman developed strategies so that these black and Hispanic students could use and further hone their mathematical and problem-solving talents. "We did not question that minority students could excel. We just wanted to know what kind of setting we would need to provide so that they could" (Treisman, 1992, p. 368). By adopting a talent development perspective and taking into account the backgrounds and characteristics of the students, Treisman and his colleagues were able to develop a model program that is responsive to the needs of a variety of students (Kuh, Douglas, Lund, and Raymin-Gyurnek, 1994).

Pedagogical Approaches. Institutions that adopt educational philosophies valuing undergraduate student learning also tend to encourage the use of such engaging pedagogies as active and collaborative learning, classroom-based problem solving, peer teaching, service learning, and various forms of electronic technologies. Other promising instructional practices are supplemental instruction, peer tutoring, reciprocal teaching, attributional retraining, concept-knowledge maps, and one-minute papers. According to Bourner (1997), the greater the repertoire of teaching methods, the more effective the learning experience, especially when teaching approaches are aligned with student abilities and preferred learning styles and learning aims. For example, if the goal is to disseminate up-to-date knowledge, lectures, guest lecturers, and use of the Internet may be effective methods. If the aim is the develop the ability to examine ideas and evaluate evidence, seminars, feedback on written work, and peer and self-assessment are preferable. In general, it is important for faculty to have high aspirations for learning outcomes, clear expectations for student performance, and standards for holding students accountable (Hassel and Lourey, 2005; Tagg, 2003).

Setting high expectations and then supporting and holding students accountable for reaching them are effective approaches for encouraging student success. High expectations for student performance characterized institutions with higher-than-predicted student engagement and graduation rates (Kuh, Kinzie, Schuh, Whitt, and Associates, 2005). According to Blose (1999), students tend to adjust their behavior and comply with the academic expectations of the environment. Although high expectations for student success should be encouraged at all institutions, Rosenbaum (1998) cautioned that it must be accompanied by realistic advice to students about degree completion and what is necessary to succeed.

Rendon (1995, 1999) champions the use of "validation"—an enabling, confirming, and supportive process initiated by faculty and other agents of socialization in and out of the classroom—to foster student success, particularly for historically underserved students. Validation activities in the teaching and learning context include addressing students by name, working one on one with students, praising students, providing encouragement and support, encouraging students to see themselves as capable of learning, and providing vehicles for students to support and praise each other. These validation actions potentially can induce "transformational changes" in students accompanied by an increased interest and confidence in their capacity to learn.

Stimulating, intellectually challenging academic tasks that demand considerable effort from students appear to be the most important influences on student growth and satisfaction, especially when buttressed by support from faculty and peers (Strauss and Volkwein, 2002; Volkwein and Cabrera, 1998). Perceptions of discrimination and prejudice in the classroom have significant negative effect on student persistence, however, particularly for minority students (Nora and Cabrera, 1996).

Faculty who are well prepared for class and design assignments that students consider meaningful have consistently positive effects on students' academic achievement and cognitive growth (Pascarella, 2001; Volkwein and others, 2000). Other instructor qualities that influence student learning include preparation and organization, clarity, availability and helpfulness, and concern for and rapport with students. As summarized by Angelo and Cross (1993) and Pascarella and Terenzini (2005):

Good teachers are knowledgeable and enthusiastic about their subject matter, encourage students to express their views through discussion, and interact with their students, both in and out of class (Feldman, 1976; Marsh, 1984; McKeachie, Pintrich, Lin, and Smith, 1986; Murray, 1985; Pascarella, 1980).

Students learn more when they are given timely feedback that is both supportive and corrective (Cross, 1987; Kulik, Kulik, and Cohen, 1980; McKeachie, Pintrich, Lin, and Smith, 1986; Menges and Mathis, 1988).

When students are expected to work hard, academic achievement, class attendance, and their sense of responsibility all increase (Berliner, 1984; Cashin, 1988; Marsh, 1984).

Because every student learns differently, individualized instruction is more effective under most circumstances (McKeachie, Pintrich, Lin, and Smith, 1986).

It seems reasonable to assume that if faculty, administrators, student affairs staff, and others who routinely interact with students outside the classroom (faculty advisors to organizations, internship supervisors, employers, peer mentors) adapted these effective approaches, out-of-class experiences would contribute more to students' learning and personal development and increase institutional productivity (Kuh, Kinzie, Schuh, Whitt, and Associates, 2005; Kuh and others, 1991). Helping faculty members acquire these skills should be a priority for faculty development programs.

Active and Collaborative Learning. Most of the scholarship on teaching and learning indicates that the passive lecture, where faculty do most of the talking and students listen, is contrary to almost every principle of an optimal learning environment (Barr and Tagg, 1995; Guskin, 1997; Tagg, 2003). Active and collaborative learning typically is more effective because students learn more when they are intensely involved in their education and are asked to think about and apply what they are learning in different settings. Collaborating with others on academic work and problem solving prepares students to deal with the messy, unscripted situations they will encounter daily during and after college (National Survey of Student Engagement, 2000) and substantially increases the amount of time and effort students spend learning (Guskin, 1997).

Problem-based or inquiry-based learning has gained a strong foothold in health science education (Allen and Duch, 1998; Duch, Gron, and Allen, 2001; Rutherford and Ahlgren, 1990). Ebert-May, Brewer, and Allred (1997) found that students learned more effectively by participating in a cooperative group; enjoyed their social interactions; characterized the classroom environment as friendly, nonthreatening, fun, and dynamic; and reported a sense of belonging and camaraderie because they regularly interacted with peers and learned from each other. Students also reported that the course had a positive impact on how hard they worked and their level of attention in class because they more frequently reported to the class about their progress on assignments. Active learning experiences also are positively associated with increased frequency of student contacts with faculty members—probably because the nature of class activities and out-of-class assignments requires it—and more positive views of the campus environment, which are probably mediated by getting to know classmates better through the collaborative exercises—all of which positively influence student integration and persistence (Braxton, Milem, and Sullivan, 2000).

In addition, participating in active learning seems to have different effects, depending on student characteristics and major field applications. For example, first-generation students who take part in group discussion, presentations, performances, research projects, and group projects, and who more frequently discuss courses with other students, had higher probability of success (Amelink, 2005). Though far from conclusive, some evidence suggests that active and collaborative learning can have compensatory effects for lower-ability students (Cruce, Wolniak, Seifert, & Pascarella, 2006; Kuh and others, 2006). When the NSSE was coadministered with several experimental learning measures, the results indicated that students who scored greater than 1300 on the SAT appeared to gain less from active and collaborative learning activities than their counterparts who scored below 990 (Carini, Kuh, and Klein, 2006). In fact, the lower-scoring group appeared to benefit more in student engagement and learning outcomes from high-quality personal relationships, a supportive campus environment, and experiences with diversity. Preferred learning styles may also be a factor. That is, "higher-ability" students may be more proficient in abstract reasoning compared with "lower-ability" students who perform better when course material is presented in concrete terms and they have opportunities to apply concepts to their daily lives. These findings are mildly provocative, suggesting that interventions to boost student engagement may have the greatest payoff for those students who are most at risk for leaving college prematurely.

Feedback. As mentioned previously, timely, appropriate feedback is positively associated with student learning and success (Chickering and Gamson, 1991; Kuh, 2003). Feedback furthers learning by providing students with guidance and information about whether they are on track in ways that enable them to change course and adjust to new circumstances and information (Kuh, Kinzie, Schuh, Whitt, and Associates, 2005; Tagg, 2003). The best feedback is interactive, involving teachers, staff, and students in a conversation about how the student is performing. Correspondingly, using classroom assessment techniques (Angelo and Cross, 1993) provides faculty members with data on teaching effectiveness and student comprehension and also involves students in active cognitive processing of information, helping them become more aware of themselves as learners (Cambridge, 1996; Steadman, 1998).

Instructional Technology. Instructional technology has matured at the same time that pedagogical approaches have expanded to serve more diverse learners (Twigg, 2002). Kuh and Hu (2001b) found that older first-year students were much less likely to use electronic technology to complete assignments or discuss course topics with peers and instructors. Those students who frequently ("often" or "very often") used information technology for classroom-related activities or assignments were more likely than their counterparts to report that their courses frequently ("quite a bit" or "very much") emphasize higher-order thinking skills, a component of academic challenge (Nelson Laird and Kuh, 2005). For example, of those students who frequently communicated with classmates online to complete academic work, 84 percent said their courses regularly emphasized applying theories or concepts to practical problems or in new situations, compared with 70 percent for those who did not frequently communicate with classmates online. Those same students also were more likely to report more frequent interactions with faculty; that is, 64 percent said they "frequently" discussed grades or assignments with an instructor, compared with only 44 percent of those who infrequently communicated with classmates online.

In addition, students who reported that their instructors frequently required using information technology were more likely to work in groups outside class more often. For example, of those students who reported that their faculty frequently used information technology in class, 59 percent indicated that they frequently work in groups outside class using the technology, compared with 41 percent of those students who said that their faculty infrequently used information technology in class.

Some evidence suggests that courses redesigned to infuse instructional technology have made the teaching and learning enterprise more active and learner centered (Twigg, 2005). Educationally effective course redesigns included instructional software and Web-based learning to engage students with course content, learning paced around mastery and modular formats, expanded support systems online and in labs, small-group activities, and alternate staffing for instructional personnel, including undergraduate peer mentors and course assistants. Course redesign projects showed improvement in course completion rates, lowered drop-failure-withdrawal rates, and higher achievement rates (Twigg, 2003).

Courses using technology, particularly those that require participation in specific experiences and on-demand support services, have been found to be positive for underserved students, especially those who are low income, first generation, and working adults (Twigg, 2005). Quality improvement techniques included online tutorials; continuous assessment and feedback, particularly in large courses moved to automated assessment; more feedback, quizzes, and online quizzing; increased interaction among students supported by the Internet; individualized on-demand support; submission of midstage drafts of papers to tutors at any time; use of computer or group learning supplemental instruction and learning centers; use of undergraduate learning assistants instead of graduate students (because undergraduate students relate better to other undergraduates); early interventions; setting baseline performance standards; and contacting those who fall behind (Twigg, 2005).

For working adult students, technology-enhanced instructional approaches afford convenience and flexibility. For example, in response to an online survey at the University of Southern Mississippi, where a large percentage of students were both low income and adult, 97 percent of the students indicated that the online materials allowed them to work on the course whenever they wanted; 91 percent said they found these materials helpful; and 85 percent disagreed or strongly disagreed with the statement, "I missed the chance to attend lecture on a regular basis." Almost all (94 percent) indicated they would like to see the online features incorporated into other courses (Twigg, 2005).

Faculty report that the use of technology in redesigned courses helped to create a more open, inclusive learning environment. Previously, students of color would not speak in class, but in the redesigned courses, they more frequently contributed while online. Both adults and students of color used the online resources for self-remediation—probably, faculty members surmise, because no one knew they were doing so. Rather than feeling stigmatized when seeking help, students could find what they needed on their own time and without anyone knowing. The learning environment at the University of Alabama, where students received individualized assistance in labs, was perceived by students seeking help to be friendlier compared with the traditional classroom, and was linked to higher performance by African American freshmen (Twigg, 2005).

Student-Centered Campus Cultures

Campuses encourage and support student learning and success by cultivating human-scale settings and an ethos of learning that pervades all aspects of the institution (Kuh, Douglas, Lund, and Ramin-Gyurnek, 1994). Learning environments with these characteristics rarely happen by accident. They almost always are intentionally designed and assiduously maintained (Kuh, Kinzie, Schuh, Whitt, and Associates, 2005; Schroeder and Hurst, 1996).

In the broadest sense, the campus environment includes the natural and physical component, a social component, an institutional component, and an "ecological-climate dimension" derived from the interaction of the other three (Conyne and Clack, 1981).

The natural and built physical environments of the campus shape behavior by permitting certain kinds of activities while limiting or making impossible other kinds (Strange and Banning, 2001). Moreover, students' commitment in terms of persistence and loyalty to the institution can be strengthened by intentionally creating a strong "sense of place" through connecting campus architecture and design to meaningful experiences and memories of activities (Kuh, Kinzie, Schuh, Whitt, and Associates, 2005). The proximity of academic buildings to student residences can promote or inhibit interactions between students from different majors (Kuh, 2000). Thus, "the actual features of the physical environment can encourage or discourage the processes of learning and development" (Strange and Banning, 2001, p. 12). Institutions vary considerably as to the degree to which their physical and social environments foster or are congenial to student success (Berger and Milem, 2000; Pascarella and Terenzini, 2005). For example, institutions can encourage student-faculty interaction and peer interaction before and after class by placing benches and comfortable seating areas near classrooms or support student-faculty interaction by creating well-equipped group study space near faculty offices, thereby increasing the likelihood of spontaneous interactions between students and faculty (Kuh, Kinzie, Schuh, Whitt, and Associates, 2005; Kuh and others, 1991).

The built environment directly affects what people with physical or visual limitations can do. Carvings, statues, paintings, and other aspects of the adapted environment value or privilege some groups over others; in some instances, members of certain groups may find some of these properties alienating—for example, portraits solely of white male campus leaders in a popular meeting room in the student center (Banning and Bartels, 1997). Understanding how various groups of students perceive and react to the physical environment should be an essential step in any effort to enhance student satisfaction and success (Banning and Cunard, 1996).

The social component represents students' demographic characteristics as well as dominant personality orientations that can be represented by the proportions of students pursuing various majors. That is, the environments of institutions with large numbers of engineering and science majors differ from those of schools with large numbers of business and performing arts students, as the personalities of the former tend to be realistic and conventional while the latter are enterprising and artistic (Holland, 1973). Smart, Feldman, and Ethington (2000) emphasize the importance of academic environment as the primary mechanism by which students further their distinctive patterns of abilities and interests. The most favorable classroom experiences, faculty interaction, and intellectual and disciplinary growth were reported by seniors majoring in departments rated high on both measures of teaching and research; students in departments that lacked a strong research climate or strong teaching climate reported less favorable experiences with faculty in and out of class (Volkwein and Carbone, 1994). Thus, a robust departmental research orientation is neither beneficial nor detrimental to students' academic experiences, but strong research combined with attention to teaching can have beneficial influence on the academic integration and intellectual growth of undergraduate majors.

Partnerships to Support Learning

Effective partnerships among those who have the most contact with students—faculty and student affairs professionals—are important to creating a campus culture that supports student success (Kuh, Kinzie, Schuh, Whitt and Associates, 2005). Institutions that have established a sense of shared responsibility for student success are characterized by a high degree of respect and collaboration among community members and have made student success important to everyone.

Powerful Partnerships: A Shared Responsibility for Learning (National Association of Student Personnel Administrators, American Association for Higher Education, and American College Personnel Association, 1998) outlines principles for sharing responsibility for student learning. *Learning Reconsidered* (National Association of Student Personnel Administrators and American College Personnel Association, 2004) promotes the integration of an institution's educational resources to develop "the whole student." One approach to cultivating effective partnerships between academic and student affairs is to work together to develop freshman interest groups (Schroeder, Minor and Tarkow, 1999). As noted earlier, freshman interest groups are designed to help students integrate and make meaning of their in-class and out-of-class experiences and encourage more frequent substantive contact with their peers and faculty members outside of class and more frequent participation in campus activities.

Designing for Diversity

Findings from research studies on diversity in college classrooms reported in *Does Diversity Make a Difference?* (American Council on Education and American Association of University Professors, 2000) demonstrate that campus diversity benefits all students. As Bauman and others (2005) emphasize, diversity should be perceived not as simply a numerical goal of a percentage of students of color but as a process toward better learning and equity in educational outcomes for all students. For example, Kuh and Umbach (2004) found that one reason students at liberal arts colleges report having more experiences with diversity is because of frequent exposure to diverse perspectives in their classes. Among the more effective ways to productively take advantage of the diversity present among students in a class is to use interactive teaching techniques such as small-group discussions, role playing, and debates and provide a supportive, inclusive classroom climate in which faculty members see themselves as learners (American Council on Education and American Association of University Professors, 2000).

Swail with Redd and Perna (2003) noted that the effectiveness of a campuswide retention program depends on supportive leadership, willingness to evoke change on campus, and careful planning. It is also important that institutional efforts to integrate students of color into predominantly white academic communities be sensitive to their needs and concerns (Eimers and Pike, 1997; Terenzini and others, 1994). Feeling a sense of fit and belonging at the institution is important because being validated by faculty, staff, and peers helps students believe they can succeed (Hernandez, 2000; Rendon, 1994a, 1999; Suarez, 2003). One of the cultural factors that may inhibit the success of African American students at PWIs is that black students spend more energy dealing with feelings of alienation and frustration as well as a lack of campus support than students at HBCUs (Watson and Kuh, 1996). Dawson-Threat (1997) found that African American men benefit from more occasions to make connections between the reality of their lives and learning experiences in the classroom. Students need safe spaces to assess, reflect on, and express their personal views, struggle with understanding human differences, and explore their identities.

A variety of institutional conditions support student success at HBCUs. The Third Black Colleges Program examined efforts designed to foster student retention, progression, and graduation and found that student retention interventions are most effective when they are integral to the college community and are a shared responsibility of many different groups in the institution (Nettles, Wagener, Millett, and Killenbeck, 1999). Because these findings have implications inside and outside the classroom, they present opportunities for collaboration between student and academic affairs.

Institutional Ethic of Improvement

Institutions focused on improving student success use information to assess their performance, pinpoint where improvement is necessary, inform change strategies, and monitor their effectiveness. Kuh, Kinzie, Schuh, Whitt, and Associates (2005) called this continuous assessment and improvement ethic "positive restlessness." Nettles, Wagener, Millett, and Killenbeck (1999) underscored the importance of developing a database for effective monitoring and evaluation to address retention, degree progression, and graduation objectives at HBCUs. For example, Bensimon's "diversity scorecard" (2004), a framework to help campuses discover and enhance their capacity to achieve comparable results for African American, Latino, and Latina students, puts data to use by establishing indicators to assess efforts to address inequities in educational outcomes. Evidence is assembled using institutional data to examine equity from four perspectives: access, retention, excellence (measurements of achievement for underrepresented students), and institutional receptivity (measures of institutional support for an affirming campus).

Summary

Institutions that foster student success provide stimulating, engaging classroom experiences that encourage students to devote more time and effort to their learning and help them develop good study habits (Kuh, Kinzie, Schuh, Whitt, and Associates, 2005; Volkwein and others, 2000). It is especially important that institutions have high-quality academic support services to meet the needs of diverse students (Bailey and Alfonso, 2005) and that student affairs and academic affairs work together to improve the learning climate inside and outside the classroom to have the greatest impact on student success. Several institutional conditions are associated with student success:

- A clear, focused institutional mission,
- High standards and expectations for student performance,
- Assessment and timely feedback,
- Student learning–centered culture,
- Peer support,
- Encouragement and support for students to explore human differences,
- Emphasis on the first college year,
- Respect for diverse ways of knowing,
- Integration of prior learning and experience,
- Academic support programs tailored to meet student needs,
- Ongoing application of learned skills,
- Active learning,
- Collaboration between student affairs and academic affairs and among students,
- An environment that emphasizes support for academic work, and
- Out-of-class contact with faculty.

The relevance of most of these conditions to student success has been demonstrated by their effective use at different types of colleges and universities across the country. For example, most institutions concentrate resources on first-year students. Other institutions have developed learning communities, which are particularly important in creating a social network for students at urban and commuter campuses. Service learning and related forms of community involvement also are widely considered educationally purposeful activities. These programs and practices are activities that institutions can put in place at relatively little additional cost and measure their impact over time on student success.

Propositions and Recommendations for Student Success in Postsecondary Education

A N ARRAY OF EDUCATIONAL POLICIES, STUDENT characteristics, institutional conditions, and other factors are associated with student success in college. This chapter offers seven propositions about what matters to student success. Taken together, the propositions represent the building blocks of a theory of student success and point to a series of complementary policies, programs, and practices that promise to enhance the performance and educational attainment of all students.

The recommendations that flow from the propositions must be adapted to fit an institution's educational mission, the characteristics of its students, and its campus culture. They must also be aligned with key elements in the external environment such as local community, state, and regional economic conditions, needs, and priorities. Equally important, the selected interventions should be demonstrably effective for the setting and student populations served and be implemented at a reasonably high level of quality. Even then, it is important to recognize that postsecondary institutions are limited in what they can do to help underprepared students overcome deficiencies in their educational preparation and other risk factors. With this in mind, we close by suggesting topics for research with the potential to improve students' chances for postsecondary success and to increase the educational effectiveness of postsecondary institutions.

Propositions and Recommendations

The trajectory for academic success in college is established long before students matriculate.

Ensure that all students have rigorous, intensive precollege academic preparation.

What students do before and during high school affects their postsecondary academic performance. As Rendon (1998, p. 61) put it, "Students begin to drop out of college in grade school." If students do not attain grade-level proficiencies—particularly in math and reading—by the eighth grade, they are much less likely to acquire the needed skills in high school, which makes early intervention even more important (Gladieux and Swail, 1998). And if students do not perform well in the right kinds of courses in high school, including four years of English and advanced mathematics classes such as algebra II, precalculus, trigonometry, and calculus, interventions later can have only modest effects on their chances to succeed and complete a baccalaureate degree.

Develop a comprehensive national college readiness strategy that addresses the educational needs of all students.

There is no substitute for rigorous academic preparation in elementary and secondary school. To markedly improve postsecondary participation and success rates in an increasingly mobile society, an unprecedented national coordinated effort is required involving communities, K–12 schools, postsecondary institutions, and local and state business leaders, government officials, and policymakers (Finn, 2006; Kirst and Venezia, 2006). Essential to this task are K–12 and postsecondary education partnerships that will strengthen the connections between various transition points—from elementary to middle school, from middle school to high school, from high school to college, and from college to work (Carnevale and Desrochers, 2003; Committee for Economic Development, 2005; Frost, 2003; McDonough, 2004; Pathways to College Network, 2004; Pennington, 2004; Venezia, Kirst, and Antonio, 2003). Although it is not realistic to presume all educational disadvantages for every student can be ameliorated, far more can be done than at present. At the same time, institutional policies and structures are needed to respond to and accommodate high-ability, highly motivated learners who can move through the system more expeditiously than currently is possible.

Toward these ends, national organizations and foundations are promoting various initiatives aimed at improving precollege experiences and shifting the societal mentality from access to college to success in college (Pathways to College Network, 2004; Venezia, Kirst, and Antonio, 2003). STAND UP is a community-based national campaign to promote better high schools. Its coalition includes public school districts, nonprofit organizations, alternative high schools, and early college high schools as well as organizations such as the New York City Department of Education, Chicago Public Schools, the National Council of La Raza, the Colorado Children's Campaign, the Knowledge Is Power Program, the Texas High School Project, and St. HOPE Public Schools in Sacramento, California. The STAND UP web site, www.standup.org, provides information for parents, guardians, and concerned citizens as well as data about the state of the nation's high schools.

The six principles in Exhibit 4 offer a glimpse of what is needed to strengthen precollege preparation (Pathways to College Network, 2004). Marketing efforts and incentives will be needed to promote and sustain the necessary collaborative efforts such as state-funded joint budget initiatives and assessment and monitoring systems that track the impact of interventions and guide continuous program improvement (Immerwahr, 2003; Pathways to College Network, 2004).

Align high school curricula with college performance standards. Many students overestimate their readiness for college, in part because state standardized tests are not articulated with college admission requirements and postsecondary academic performance expectations. Fortunately, efforts to reform standards are gaining momentum. Standards for Success, a project sponsored by the AAC&U with funding from The Pew Charitable Trusts, has developed tools to help guide these alignment efforts (Conley, 2003) and is a good source for learning what is required from schools, communities, and postsecondary faculty and staff members.

Provide incentives in state budgets to increase the number of students who become college ready in high school and enroll in college.

State budgets do not provide incentives for efforts to promote college readiness in high school (Kirst and Venezia, 2006). One option is for states to offer incentives to local school districts to provide dual enrollment opportunities to

EXHIBIT 4
Principles for Strengthening Precollege Preparation

- Principle One: Expect that all underserved students are capable of being prepared to enroll and succeed in college. Set high expectations for all students.
- Principle Two: Provide a range of high-quality college preparatory tools for underserved students and their families.
  - Require a complete college-preparatory core curriculum.
  - Make honors and college-credit courses available to all students.
  - Provide early college awareness programs and broad support services to accelerate student learning.
  - Make language-accessible college planning and financial aid information available.
- Principle Three: Embrace social, cultural, and learning style differences in developing learning environments and activities for underserved students.
  - Involve families in supporting learning.
  - Affirm students' social and cultural backgrounds.
  - Create environments that support diversity and foster positive intergroup relations.
- Principle Four: Involve leaders at all levels in establishing policies, programs, and practices that facilitate student transitions toward postsecondary attainment:
  - From elementary to middle school
  - From middle to high school
  - From high school to college
  - From college to work and further education.
- Principle Five: Provide sufficient financial and human resources to enable underserved students to prepare for, enroll, and succeed in college.
  - Staff schools and programs with well-qualified teachers, counselors, and leaders.
  - Ensure equitable funding that addresses past deficiencies and meets student needs.
  - Adequately fund need-based financial aid.
- Principle Six: Assess policy, program, practice, and institutional effectiveness regularly.
  - Use assessment models that demonstrate whether practices are working for underserved students.
  - Collect and use data that provide feedback for continuous improvement.
  - Employ a variety of analytical tools.

Source: Pathways to College Network, 2004.

high school students and to schools where students who go on to college do not require postsecondary remediation. Such a program would require alignment between high school and college academic standards and an integrated K–16 finance model (Kirst and Venezia, 2006).

Instill in K–12 educators an assets-based talent development philosophy about teaching and learning.

Sadly, high school teachers have lower educational aspirations for their students than students themselves or their parents (U.S. Department of Education, 2003b). These deleterious beliefs and assumptions about students and their learning—those that teachers hold and those that students have about themselves—must be changed. Then students must be held to high standards to ensure they acquire the skills and competencies demanded in college. Teachers must adapt their instructional approaches to accommodate their students' different learning styles to build on students' assets and strengths rather than initially dwelling on shortcomings (Dweck, 2000). Teacher education and educational leadership programs are key to preparing professional educators who subscribe to an "assets view" of their students. Shifting the cultures of K–12 schools to encourage teachers and administrators to approach students and families in this way is challenging and will likely require foundation support and local and state incentives over many years to fully realize the goal.

Family and community support are indispensable to raising a student's educational aspirations, becoming college prepared, and persisting.

Increase the quality of information to students and families who lack adequate information about going to college, including real costs and availability of aid.

Before the 1990s, much of the discussion regarding access and educational attainment focused on the academic preparation of students and financial aid policies (St. John, 2003; Tierney, Corwin, and Colyar, 2005; Tierney and Hagedorn, 2002; Wilkinson, 2005). More recently, it has become clear that too many students, especially those from historically underserved backgrounds, lack accurate information about postsecondary options. They are confused about expectations for academic work, actual tuition costs, and the content of college entrance and placement tests (Venezia, Kirst, and Antonio, 2003).

Every high school student and family must be made aware of the "million dollar decision"—the financial cost over a lifetime of not completing a postsecondary degree (Pennington, 2004). Students most at risk tend to have less accurate information about college and get less encouragement and support from their family and friends for preparing for and attending college. Like many of the other large-scale initiatives, partnerships between school personnel and neighborhood or community and educational agencies are essential to make certain parents and other family members obtain the information and understand how to adequately prepare for college and the importance of family support.

For example, the substantial body of research on college choice shows that the timing, quality, and quantity of information provided to students about postsecondary educational opportunities can help raise and clarify their educational aspirations (Hossler, Schmit, and Vesper, 1999). Students begin to become interested in different postsecondary options in the tenth grade, and this interest builds during the eleventh and twelfth grades. Thus *sophomores* in high school should start receiving information about various types of post-secondary schools and admissions requirements. Many sophomores, however, do not actively seek out information and are not aware of the types of assistance available to help them think about pursuing a postsecondary education (Schmit, 1991). Taking the PSAT and the SAT and completing the Free Application for Federal Student Aid cause students and their families to think more carefully about postsecondary education. Sometime in the spring or summer of the junior year, students thinking about attending a four-year institution become more interested in receiving information about postsecondary options (Kinzie and others, 2004). At this stage, they start to read the information that colleges send them and even begin to seek out additional information.

McDonough (2004) reported that students who participated in well-designed early intervention programs had had most of the information needed to prepare for college. National initiatives such as the nonprofit National College Access Network, which supports a network of state and local college access programs providing counseling, advice, and financial assistance to students and families, can help open the doors of postsecondary education through counseling and support. State and other local initiatives such as College Mentors for Kids! Inc., which cultivates ongoing one-on-one relationships between college and elementary-aged students through shared experiences on the campus and in the community, and Learn More Resource Center (formerly the Indiana College Placement and Assessment Center), under the direction of the Indiana Commission for Higher Education, are models for state-level dissemination of information about college.

Expand the scale and scope of demonstrably effective college encouragement and transition programs.

Postsecondary encouragement programs have emerged in every state in recent years to help improve access for students from low- and moderate-income families as well as first-generation students (Hossler, Schmit, and Vesper, 1999; Tierney, Corwin, and Colyar, 2005; Tierney and Hagedorn, 2002). Parental involvement and college outreach programs seem to be particularly effective. For example, several high-profile programs in California that serve largely Hispanic populations such as the Parent Institute for Quality Education and the Puente Project have successfully brought together Latino families, students, teachers, and counselors to learn more about postsecondary options and financial aid (Chrispeels and Rivero, 2001; Pathways to College Network, 2004).

GEAR UP, one of the largest and best-funded initiatives, provides information about financial aid, family support and counseling, and tutoring, among other things (Hossler and Schmit, 1995; St. John, 2003; Tierney and Hagedorn, 2002). GEAR UP was based in part on an Indiana early encouragement program, Twenty-First Century Scholars (TFCS), which provides financial assistance and support to students from lower-income families to encourage participation in postsecondary education (Hossler, Schmit, and Vesper, 1999). Despite the fact that TFCS pays the tuition and fees at four-year public institutions for students who complete the program, however, many eligible students do not enroll in TFCS, and fewer than 60 percent of those who enroll matriculate to postsecondary institutions after high school graduation. Many reasons related to status attainment, social reproduction, and habitus partially explain this disappointing number, ranging from reluctance to leave home for students from small rural communities to neighborhood violence to a lack of confidence and competence in moving to another world (D. Hossler, personal communication, March 11, 2006). In short, money, better preparation, and some information about college cannot make up for years of relative cultural, educational, and social deprivation.

Other promising initiatives to encourage students include many of the TRIO programs funded under Title IV of the Higher Education Act such as Upward Bound, Upward Bound Math/Science, Student Support Services, Talent Search, Educational Opportunity Center, and the McNair Program (Institute for Higher Education Policy, 1995, 2001; Pathways to College Network, 2004). For example, students in the Upward Bound program are four times more likely to earn an undergraduate degree. Students in TRIO Student Support Services programs are more than twice as likely to remain in college as those students from similar backgrounds who did not participate in the program (http://www.trioprograms.org/abouttrio.html). Students with the lowest educational aspirations and those who participate longer tend to benefit the most. For example, for each additional year of Upward Bound completed, the chances increase by 9 percent that the student will attend a postsecondary institution (Meyers and others, 2004; Muraskin, 1997). Programs such as the Intensive Freshman Seminar and Groups Program at Indiana University Bloomington with a strong residential component are among the more effective, allowing students to become familiar with the physical, social, and cultural environments of the campus where they will matriculate (Barovick and Baron, 2001).

Credit-based transition programs such as tech-prep, dual or concurrent enrollment, international baccalaureate, and middle college high schools allow high school students to take college-level classes for college credit (Hughes, Karp, Fermin, and Bailey, 2005). Nationally, approximately 57 percent of postsecondary institutions in thirty-eight states have dual enrollment programs (Hoffman, 2005; Kleiner and Lewis, 2005). Some of them are geared to talented students, others are geared to students who need academic enrichment, and others are open to anyone who is interested in getting a head start on college. Pennington (2004) suggests a number of other innovative interventions such as accelerating progress through grades eleven through fourteen by moving toward competency-based models; introducing more choice and competition in the system where high schools, private schools, community colleges, and universities compete for students; and expanding learning options during the summer. Terenzini, Springer, and others (1996) also suggested such work- or high-school-to-college transition programs can provide the types of validating experiences first-generation students need for a successful college transition.

Another promising intervention is supplemental education, the formal and informal learning and development opportunities that occur outside the regular school day (Bridglall and Gordon, 2002). Gordon (1999) found that this type of approach—whether from home computers, parents and siblings, libraries, mentoring and tutoring programs, peer-based study groups, or faith-based activities—created an experience similar to that of an engaging learning community.

The right amount and kind of money matters to student success; too little can make it impossible for students to pay college bills, while too much loan debt can discourage students from persisting.
Align financial aid and tuition policy so that financial assistance packages meet students' need.

Affordability depends on many factors, including the state of the economy and the amount of aid available to students from state systems and individual institutions (Finney and Kelly, 2004). Believing that college is within reach financially is a major obstacle for many historically underserved students. About nine of ten college-qualified low-income students had an annual unmet financial need averaging less than $5,000. If this figure is accurate, it seems to be a manageable amount of debt to incur when compared with the long-term benefits. Even so, convincing loan-averse families to take on additional debt to pay for college is not a trivial matter. These very real concerns notwithstanding, financial support to attend college must be made available in amounts and forms that enable low-income students to attend full time rather than part time and—when necessary—work fewer hours, preferably on campus rather than off campus.

One plan that promises to redress inequities in how aid is distributed to different groups of students is the Changing Directions project funded by Lumina Foundation for Education and coordinated by the Western Interstate Commission for Higher Education with collaboration from the State Higher Education Executive Officers and the American Council on Education (Heller, 2002; Western Interstate Commission for Higher Education, 2003). At first blush, equalizing need-based financial aid awards seems easy to accomplish, but very few states have done so; Minnesota's Design for Shared Responsibility is one of the few working models. This initiative sets no arbitrary family income limits, and students can use state aid to attend full or part time at public or private institutions. Another proposal, the Student's Total Education Package put forth by the National Commission on Responsibilities for Financing Post-Secondary Education (Institute for Higher Education Policy, 1995), would make all full-time undergraduate college students eligible for the same maximum amount of federal aid, with the type of aid depending on financial need and institutional cost. The poorest students would receive primarily grants, work-study assistance, and subsidized loans. Students from middle-income families could receive a mix of subsidized and unsubsidized loans, work-study assistance, and grants. Students from affluent families would not be eligible for subsidized aid but could receive an unsubsidized loan. Such policies would make plain the exact amount and packaging of aid students could receive from the federal government, thereby reducing some confusion and uncertainly.

Create small pockets of emergency funds to address real student needs in "real" time.

Providing even small amounts of money at key times can mean the difference between some students staying in school or leaving. For example, some students drop out because they do not have enough money at the beginning of the academic term to buy books. Most institutions can find additional resources to expand their short-term emergency loans to address this issue. But first the institution must recognize the problem and then act expeditiously. This solution will require cooperation from academic and student affairs leaders and logistical support from financial aid and academic advising personnel.

Most students—especially those who start college with two or more characteristics associated with premature departure—benefit from early interventions and sustained attention at key transition points. *Clarify institutional values and expectations early and often to prospective and matriculating students.*

Colleges and universities have two nonnegotiable obligations to their students. The first is to establish expectations for high performance inside and outside the classroom appropriate to students' abilities and aspirations. To do so, a school must first understand who its students are, what they are prepared to do academically, and what they expect of the institution and themselves.

- What are the expectations first-year students from different backgrounds have for college?
- What factors account for different levels of expectations among first-year students?
- What role do students' expectations play in shaping their actual experiences and perceptions of the campus environment?

The second obligation institutions have to their students is to give them prompt, frequent feedback about how well they are meeting these expectations. A substantial number of new students may not fully understand and appreciate their role as learners. Far fewer students use campus learning and support services than say they will when starting college (National Survey of Student Engagement, 2005). To address these concerns, faculty members, advisors, and student affairs professionals must clearly and consistently communicate to students what is expected and provide periodic feedback as to the quality of students' performance.

Provide multiple, interconnected learning support networks, early warning systems, and safety nets.

Students attending institutions that employ a comprehensive system of complementary initiatives based on effective educational practices are more likely to perform better academically, be more satisfied, and persist and graduate. Among these initiatives are those described in the previous chapter such as well-designed and -implemented orientation, placement testing, first-year seminars, learning communities, intrusive advising, early warning systems, redundant safety nets, supplemental instruction, peer tutoring and mentoring, theme-based campus housing, adequate financial aid including on-campus work, internships, service learning, and demonstrably effective teaching practices (Forest, 1985, Kuh, Kinzie, Schuh, Whitt, and Associates, 2005; Wang and Grimes, 2001). Simply offering such programs and practices does not guarantee that they will have the intended effects on student success, however; institutional programs and practices must be of high quality, customized to meet the needs of students they are intended to reach, and firmly rooted in a student success–oriented campus culture (Kuh, Kinzie, Schuh Whitt, and Associates, 2005).

Waiting until midterm examinations is often too late to give students an idea of how well they are performing. Advisors and academic support program personnel do some of their most important work by paying attention to student class attendance patterns, drop and add information, early semester and midterm grades, and preregistration information. Some institutions, Truman State among them, have used the College Student Expectations Questionnaire or the Beginning College Student Survey of Student Engagement to help students see how their in-class and out-of-class activities compare with those of their peers in terms of study time, talking with faculty members about various matters, and participation in cocurricular activities, to name a few. Faculty members teaching in Fayetteville State University's Early Alert program contact first-year student mentors and University College to alert them about students experiencing difficulty during the first two weeks of the semester. Mentors contact students to advise and refer as appropriate. At Wheaton College in Massachusetts, a first-year student's "advising team" is made up of a faculty member, a student preceptor, a librarian, and a staff member. These and other approaches adapted to local conditions and student characteristics are needed at every institution.

Concentrate early intervention resources on those who have two or more risk factors.

Underprepared first-generation students and ethnic minorities are especially at risk, particularly those from lower income levels and those who have one or more of the other risk factors listed in Exhibit 1. At some institutions, additional risk factors may come into play, depending on the nature of students' ability to pay for college, the curriculum, and campus climate. Thus, interventions are needed both before and during college for these students.

Students who find something or someone worthwhile to connect to in the postsecondary environment are more likely to engage in educationally purposeful activities, persist, and achieve their educational objectives.

Make the classroom the locus of community.

Many commuter students spend only a limited amount of time on campus. The classroom is the only regular point of contact they have with other students (including those who are not in their primary reference groups) and with faculty and staff members. Thus using the classroom to create communities of learning must be a high priority in terms of creating a success-oriented campus culture. Faculty members in partnership with student affairs professionals and other staff familiar with culture-building strategies can work together to fashion a rich, engaging classroom experience that complements the institution's academic values and students' preferred learning styles. Thus faculty members must also be more intentional about teaching institutional values and traditions and informing students about campus events, procedures, and deadlines such as registration. In addition, faculty members could design cooperative learning activities that bring students together to work together after class on meaningful tasks.

Structure ways for more commuter students to spend time with classmates.

Because peers are very influential on student learning and the development of values, institutions must harness and shape this influence to the extent possible so it is educationally purposeful and helps to reinforce academic expectations. A well-designed first-year seminar, freshman interest group, or learning community can serve this purpose (Matthews, 1994; Muraskin, 2003; Price, 2005; Tinto, 1996, 2004; Tinto, Love, and Russo, 1995). One version of the first-year seminar used at different types of colleges and universities is University 101 developed at the University of South Carolina, which is primarily focused on orienting students to college and teaching survival and academic success skills. Another variation is to organize academic offerings in the first year so that all first-year students have at least one discipline-based course with twenty-five or fewer students taught by a faculty member. An especially attractive approach is for the seminar instructor to serve as the academic advisor for the students in the seminar for the first college year. Such seminars will be more fulfilling for students as well as instructors if the latter are provided a structured opportunity to prepare and reflect periodically on their experiences in the company of colleagues.

Involve every student in a meaningful way in some activity or with a positive role model in the college environment.

Working on campus, writing for the student newspaper, or conducting research with a faculty member can be a life-changing experience. When students are required to take responsibility for activities that require daily decisions and tasks, they become invested in the activity and more committed to the college and their studies. Advisors, counselors, and others who have routine contact with students must persuade or otherwise induce them to get involved with one or more of these kinds of activities or people (such as faculty or staff members). For example, upper-division students at the University of Michigan who were involved in the undergraduate research program in their first year of college described continued and meaningful contact with their faculty mentors (Kuh, Kinzie, Schuh, Whitt, and Associates, 2005). Academic advisors must also encourage students to become involved with peers in campus events and organizations and invest effort in educational activities known to promote student learning and development (Braxton and McClendon, 2001–02).

Encourage students to live on campus—at least for the first year—at institutions where housing available. Students living on campus represent only about 15 percent of all undergraduates, so this recommendation applies to a relatively small number of students at institutions with campus housing available. Yet the fact remains that students who live on campus are more engaged and gain more from their college experience. They have easier access to faculty and staff members and peers, and they are more likely to take advantage of the institution's cultural and artistic venues. They also have more experiences with diversity. If an institution wants to improve first-generation student success rates, it should create ways to make it possible for those students to live on campus, at least for the first year. For low-income, first-generation students, such a policy will require additional financial assistance. Work-study or co-op living units could be created to offset cost differences between living on and off campus or at home. For older students with families and full-time jobs, it is not an option, so innovative approaches are needed that attract nontraditional students and their families to spend time on the campus.

Institutions that focus on student success, subscribe to a talent development philosophy, and create a student-centered culture are better positioned to help their students attain their educational objectives.

Instill in postsecondary educators an asset-based talent development philosophy about teaching and learning.

As with K–12 teachers and staff, the debilitating beliefs and assumptions about student learning held by postsecondary instructors must be also changed (Dweck, 2000). More than a few colleges and universities have woven this philosophy into their cultures (Chickering, 2006; Kuh, Kinzie, Schuh, Whitt, and Associates, 2005). For example, many MSIs operate from an asset-based philosophy for student learning. Some MSIs, including California State University, Monterey Bay, Fayetteville State University, Spelman College, University of Texas at El Paso, Winston-Salem State University, and Xavier University, provide well-integrated and redundant opportunities for students to engage with their peers in important educational practices, including active and collaborative learning and service learning. In addition, certain HBCUs appear to connect students and faculty in ways that increase students' level of engagement and commitment to success. This combination of clarity of mission, talent development, and supportive campus climate helps these institutions to overcome substantial financial and physical plant inequalities to foster student success (Kuh, Kinzie, Schuh, Whitt, and Associates, 2005). Creating these affirming conditions for learning has implications for K–12 teacher preparation programs, graduate education (where the next generation of college instructors is being prepared), and faculty development efforts in postsecondary settings.

Use effective educational practices throughout the institution.

Postsecondary institutions can address shortcomings in students' academic preparation and increase the chances that students will succeed by adapting demonstrably effective policies and practices. How and why many of these practices work in different institutional settings with different types of students was discussed in the previous chapter (see also Chickering and Gamson, 1987; Chickering and Reisser, 1993; Education Commission of the States, 1995; Kuh, Douglas, Lund, and Ramin-Gyurnek, 1994; Kuh, Kinzie, Schuh, Whitt, and Associates, 2005; Kuh and others, 1991; Pascarella and Terenzini, 2005). Other promising practices specific to particular groups or activities also are available, such as working with adult learners (Cook and King, 2005), undergraduate teaching and learning (Sorcinelli, 1991), developmental education for underprepared students (Boyland, 2002; Grubb, 2001), assessment (AAHE, 1992), and student affairs work (Blimling and Whitt, 1999).

Use technology in educationally effective ways.

The evaluative data from Program in Course Redesign (Twigg, 2005) suggest that when used appropriately, information technology can be a solution rather than an obstacle to increasing success for underserved students. A key step is ensuring learners' readiness to benefit from technology-based courses. Readiness involves more than access to computers. It also involves having access to technical support and other forms of support—such as help in using navigation tools and course management systems—and the processes that enable students to gain literacy skills if they do not already possess them.

Give institutions incentives to identify and ameliorate debilitating cultural properties.

Policy and programmatic interventions are necessary but insufficient to shift a campus to a student success paradigm. Kuh, Kinzie, Schuh, Whitt, and Associates (2005) describe different types of educational policies and practices and offer recommendations for how to cultivate and sustain student-friendly campus cultures (see also Kuh, Douglas, Lund, and Ramin-Gyurnek, 1994; Kuh and others, 1991). These efforts are especially important for promoting the success of historically underserved students because their premature departure is partly the result of their inability to successfully navigate the distance and differences between their cultures of origin and the institution's dominant culture (Kuh and Love, 2000). Students either reject the institution's attempt to socialize them or they have not found a cultural enclave from which they can draw support and guidance as they try to negotiate what seems to be an alien culture

(Attinasi, 1989; Tierney, 1992). One approach is to physically and symbolically link families to the campus (Ortiz, 2004; Torres, 2003). Possible strategies include involving students in community-based experiential learning activities and providing students and their families opportunities to visit campus before and after matriculation to develop a sense of the support systems available to students on campus. Rather than trying to force continued cultural distinctions between life at home and at college, the goal is to create a "mestiza consciousness" (Anzaldua, 1987) that melds these seemingly opposed worlds in a mutually satisfying way. Whatever is tried, efforts to create hospitable campus climates for diverse student populations must be culturally sensitive to understand and ameliorate the ways that dominant values, norms, and practices may contribute to perceptions of a hostile environment for students whose backgrounds differ from the majority (Berger, 2000; Kuh and others, 1991).

Focus assessment and accountability efforts on what matters to student success.

Periodically examine the student experience, inside and outside the classroom.

Many campuses know a good deal about their first-year students and graduating seniors. More must also be learned about those students who leave college without completing their degree, especially those who are only a semester or two away from fulfilling graduation requirements. The students at greatest risk of leaving college sometime after the second year are almost identical in terms of demographic characteristics with those who leave before that point. Because socialization to academic norms is not complete at the end of the first year of college, especially for first-generation college students and others who lack knowledge about what is required to succeed at the university or whose goals and aspirations are not yet clear, additional interventions may be needed for certain groups so that these students continue to engage in the kinds of activities associated with success in college.

Provide incentives for postsecondary institutions to responsibly report and use information about the student experience to improve teaching, learning, and personal development.

A variety of excellent assessment tools are available to provide useful information that institutions can use. Certainly more need to be developed. The results of these assessments must be analyzed, interpreted, and reported in responsible ways that take into account the diversity of student backgrounds and abilities as well as institutional missions and resources. Whatever measures are used, they should be calculated separately for groups of students with different background characteristics such as race, ethnicity, gender, SES, first-generation status, and transfer status. Such analyses may raise nettlesome questions. For example, when evaluating the quality of the educational experience, how much responsibility for transfer students' performance belongs to the institution, to the individual student, and to the other institutions transfer students have attended? This assignment of responsibility is especially important, given that three-fifths of baccalaureate degree recipients attend two or more colleges and as many as one-quarter take classes at two or more different schools in the same academic term.

At colleges committed to student success, people constantly remind themselves of their pursuit of excellence by periodically reviewing campus priorities, policies, and practices to ensure that what is enacted is of acceptable quality and consistent with the institution's espoused priorities and values (Kuh, Kinzie, Schuh, Whitt, and Associates, 2005). Such examinations are sometimes formal such as program reviews or accreditation self-studies. For example, the University of Michigan conducted six major studies of the quality of the undergraduate experience between the mid-1980s and 2000.

Provide incentives for postsecondary institutions to adopt a common reporting template for indicators of student success to make their performance transparent.

We value what we measure. One way to bring about more transparency in student and institutional performance is to develop a common template that schools can use to display their performance results. A one-size-fits-all set of indicators will not likely be sufficient, given the increasing diversity of college students and the multiple, winding pathways they follow to a baccalaureate degree. Multiple sets of indicators will be needed to yield an accurate, albeit more complicated, picture of the student experience and to document various measures of success for different types of institutions and students. Along with student engagement data, other commonly used indicators of success include student retention and graduation. Other outcomes of interest include student goal attainment, course retention, transfer rates and transfer success, success in subsequent coursework, fall-to-fall persistence, degree or certificate completion, student satisfaction, student personal and professional development, citizenship and student involvement, student learning outcomes, and postcollege outcomes, including graduate school, employment, and lifelong learning. The Carnegie Foundation for the Advancement of Teaching recently introduced additional criteria for grouping institutions with similar students and educational purposes and offerings. A "student success organizing framework" that takes into account student and institutional characteristics in addition to mission and academic programs would be a welcome addition and allow policymakers, state governments, parents, and other groups to compare the performance of similar types of schools for various purposes.

Further develop state and institutional capacity for collecting, analyzing, and using data to improve accountability.

One of the most powerful levers for institutional improvement is the use of credible data that tell a more comprehensive story of students' educational experiences in our colleges and universities. To do so requires an expanded technological and human capacity for data collection and analysis, an extraordinarily wide range of which—from paper-and-pencil operations conducted by part-time faculty members to highly sophisticated research operations—is available across states and institutions. Until colleges, universities, and state systems have the capacity to routinely track longitudinally student cohorts, regularly elicit responses from students on surveys and other assessments, and *use* that data to engage faculty and student service professionals in discussions about strengths and needs for improvement, our ability to prompt significant institutional change will be severely limited. It is therefore important to build adequate data systems.

Needed Research

The foregoing propositions represent what the literature points to as conditions that matter to student success. As with most complicated matters in a dynamic, even volatile, environment (Association of American Colleges and Universities, 2007), additional research is needed to better understand various aspects of student performance before and during college to develop a comprehensive theory of student success (Pascarella and Terenzini, 2005; Social

Science Research Council Project, 2005; Tinto, 2004). This section proposes some research and development activities that can address some of the gaps in our understanding of the factors that contribute to student success.

Determine the more effective approaches for encouraging different types of students (for example, first generation, low income, students of color, men) to participate in and benefit from postsecondary encouragement programs.

In the absence of incontrovertible evidence of what works, it is difficult to persuade policymakers and institutional leaders to allocate scarce resources to postsecondary encouragement and access initiatives. Among the programs we need to learn more about are dual-enrollment programs, middle college–early college schools where students attain sufficient college credit while in high school to graduate with a high school diploma and an associate's degree or two years of transferable college credit (Middle College National Consortium, 2006), vocational-technical policies and innovations, bridge programs, and P–16 initiatives. We also need to know which of these programs and their variants work with students who are less likely to become college ready and enroll such as low-income students, men, and students of color. To be eligible for many of these programs, students must take certain steps, which they and their families may be unaware of, such as meeting certain academic standards (Bishop, 2002, 2004) or pledging to stay drug free. We need to know who takes advantage of these programs (or not) and their effects on student persistence and educational outcomes. The absence of longitudinal K–16 data, the inability of states to track students through the pipeline, institutional review and privacy issues, and other security problems all hamper our ability to effectively analyze and interpret precollege research and interventions (Venezia, Kirst, and Antonio, 2003).

Develop additional ways to assess the ability to do college-level work.

Sternberg (2005) contends that students from lower-SES backgrounds often have substantial hidden talents that are not reflected in traditional college screening tools such as the ACT or SAT or high school grades, necessitating the need for other measures that assess analytical, creative, and practical skills. Another approach is to evaluate the efficacy of the SAT merit index to predict success in college. The merit index subtracts the average SAT test score for an individual's high school from the student's individual test score, providing an estimate of the extent to which a student's ability exceeded what could be reasonably expected, given the student's academic environment (St. John, Hu, Simmons, and Musoba, 1999). These and other tools may yield more useful assessments of an individual's talent, ability, and motivation to do college-level work.

Identify efficient ways for colleges and universities to report back to high schools their graduates' college performance and use the information.

For high schools to better prepare their students for the academic challenges presented in postsecondary education, teachers and administrators must know how their graduates perform in postsecondary settings so they can modify and strengthen the high school curriculum (American Diploma Project, 2004; Conley, 2003). Although some systems are in place such as California State University's Collaborative Academic Preparation Initiative (Roach, 2000), too often high schools and community agencies do not have the means to effectively gather and use this information to improve student preparation.

Evaluate the performance of each state's educational system.

The National Center on Public Policy and Higher Education's biennial state-by-state report card presents revealing data, but they are gross indicators of the current state of affairs in key performance categories. Little information points to what states, K–12 schools, or postsecondary institutions can and should do to *improve* their performance. More fine-grained analyses are needed that can help answer several questions:

- What types of students leave the educational system at which junctures?
- Are current interventions addressing the proximal causes of student departure at these points?
- Are early warning systems and assessment tools adequate for the task of identifying these students early enough to intervene?
- Are aid programs working as intended?
- How do changes in tuition and financial aid policy affect enrollment and persistence?
- Do students carefully consider their postsecondary options at the appropriate time?
- Which transition points need more attention?

Determine the most efficient way of using financial aid to encourage student preparation for college and to make college affordable for students who need financial support to attend college.

Loans seem to be helpful in encouraging white students to persist but do not positively affect completion rates for African American and Latino students. Price sensitivity and family views of different kinds of financial aid are also key factors. In addition to having enough money available to make college appear to be affordable and actually to be affordable, we need to know more about what types of aid packages under what circumstances encourage students to become ready, apply, enroll, and complete college.

Develop additional indicators of success for different types of institutions and students.

Determining reasonable institutional indicators of student success must involve a variety of groups—policymakers, administrators, faculty, staff, and students. Commonly used indicators of success include student retention and graduation. To be sensitive to diverse types of institutions and students, we need to develop valid, reliable measures of student goal attainment, course retention, transfer rates and transfer success, success in subsequent coursework, fall-to-fall persistence, degree or certificate completion, student satisfaction, student personal and professional development, citizenship and student involvement, student learning outcomes, and postcollege outcomes, including graduate school, employment, and lifelong learning (see Appendix B). For example, measures of success in subsequent coursework are important measures for students who have been historically underrepresented in specific majors and at institutions that provide remedial education. Agreeing about what are legitimate indicators will not be easy, because so many groups from state and federal policymakers to business leaders to institutional officials have an interest in the issue.

Determine appropriate, responsible ways to measure, report, and use student success indicators for purposes of accountability and improvement.

Persistence rates appear to have risen between the early and mid-1990s, though there was no perceptible change in graduation rates (Horn and Berger, 2004). This finding suggests that this cohort of students may be persisting longer and attending multiple institutions on the road to the baccalaureate.

Thus it is possible that current estimates of educational attainment rates are higher than typically reported. Accurate, real-time, state-level tracking systems and data sharing across states are needed to paint a comprehensive, more accurate picture of persistence and graduation rates. States such as Florida, Ohio, and Texas have made good progress in this regard (P. Ewell, personal communication, January 11, 2006).

Using instruments such as the CCSSE and the NSSE is one relatively inexpensive approach that can serve multiple purposes (assessment, accountability, improvement). Another approach is systematically auditing the extent to which conditions for student success exist such as described in the Inventory for Student Engagement and Success (Kuh, Kinzie, Schuh, Whitt, and Associates, 2005). Does the organization and delivery of the curriculum facilitate or present obstacles to student success? A problem common to many universities is the gateway mathematics course that some majors require where the traditional approach to delivering course content *assumes* that not all students can master challenging mathematical concepts. As a result, a substantial number of students do not master the material, impeding their progress to degree. At Indiana University Bloomington several years ago, more than a third of the students in a particular math course in a given term typically received a D or F grade or withdrew from the class. The math faculty redesigned this one-semester course and, among other things, created a reduced pace two-semester offering that covers the same material and uses the same exams. Several years later, the percentage of students who now complete the course with a C or better jumped by about 20 percent (Hossler, Kuh, and Olsen, 2001).

Verify the institutional policies and practices that work best with different groups of students (low income, first generation, ethnic minorities, immigrants, men, and so forth) at different types of institutions (two-year and four-year colleges, public and private schools, and private for-profit entities).

Single-institution and consortia studies are needed to learn more about which interventions are effective with different groups of students at different points in time. Who is most likely to benefit from remediation, and what are the costs and benefits of various remediation approaches? Are pedagogical approaches that feature active and collaborative learning activities appropriate for all students? Do all students who report more experience with such activities learn more and graduate at higher rates than their counterparts? Engaging pedagogies such as active and collaborative learning and electronic technology that permit instructors to offer just-in-time assistance to students who are having difficulty mastering concepts offer great promise for increasing student learning and keeping students motivated to complete learning tasks and to persist. Although engaging teaching approaches appear to be more or less effective with all students (National Survey of Student Engagement, 2005), we need to discover whether some approaches work better with students with certain characteristics than others.

Determine the elements of institutional culture at different types of postsecondary settings that are associated with student success.

Virtually every study of high-performing organizations concludes that culture is a major factor in their success (Collins, 2001; Kuh, Kinzie, Schuh, Whitt, and Associates, 2005; Kuh and Whitt, 1988; Tierney, 1999). Particularly instructive would be studies of the institutional conditions associated with student success at community colleges, special mission institutions, and MSIs that control for student precollege characteristics such as first-generation status, SES, aspirations, and academic preparation (Becker and Andrews, 2004; Fitzgerald, 2004; Heller, 2004; Swail, Cabrera, Lee, and Williams, 2005). Another understudied area is how organizational structures at colleges affect student performance and satisfaction. Learning more about how students make sense of and navigate the college environment has greater potential to reveal aspects of the organizational structure that support and hinder student success.

The research on student development indicates that students learn more and more deeply when their experiences inside and outside the classroom are complementary and mutually reinforcing. Many institutions are doing exemplary work in this area (see, for example, Kuh, Kinzie, Schuh, Whitt, and Associates, 2005; Kuh and others, 1991). More studies of such efforts would be welcome, particularly those that discover and describe programs and practices at institutions that enroll large numbers of part-time and commuting students, as this segment of students will continue to increase. Such efforts would also help us better understand the "invisible tapestry" (Kuh and Whitt, 1988) of language, norms, and other cultural properties that contribute to student success.

Examine the educational effectiveness of private, for-profit postsecondary institutions.

Very little is known about the student experiences at these types of institutions, which have rapidly increasing enrollments. As a result, it is not possible to determine what role they play in the educational system in terms of enhancing student learning and contributing to the educational capital of the state and nation.

Examine the motivations and quality of educational experiences of students attending multiple institutions. The "swirl" phenomenon—attending two or more postsecondary schools in a meandering pattern or concurrent enrollment at two or more schools in the same academic term—is a fact of contemporary college attendance. Very little is known about the experiences of these students, even though they now account for the majority of all undergraduates who earn a bachelor's degree. We need more and better information about institutional attendance patterns (including transfer students) and their effects on student learning and other indicators of student success.

Determine what postsecondary institutions can realistically do and at what cost to help academically underprepared students overcome the deficiencies they bring with them to college.

The weight of the evidence shows that precollege experiences— especially taking the right kinds of courses in high school—are key to persistence and graduation. Given this hard truth, how much can postsecondary institutions realistically be expected to do? Although much of the solution to student success in college is related to the quality of precollege academic preparation, postsecondary institutions must do everything feasible to help their students who matriculate without the requisite skills and competencies to perform at a satisfactory level. Systematic efforts are needed to determine the design and delivery of advising and counseling services and developmental coursework that are effective with different types of learners in different types of settings. The results of such inquiries can help to establish realistic benchmarks that policymakers, funding agencies, and institutional leaders can use for purposes of accountability and institutional improvement.

A Final Word

Earning a bachelor's degree is linked to long-term cognitive, social, and economic benefits to individuals, benefits that are passed on to future generations, enhancing the quality of life of the families of college-educated persons, the communities where they live, and the larger society. Although college was once considered an option for a relatively small percentage of the adult population, it no longer is. Indeed, the majority of adults—perhaps more than 80 percent—needs some form of postsecondary education to live and work productively in a rapidly changing, information-based economy. For this reason, various groups have put forward scores of policy recommendations for how policymakers, states, K–12 schools, postsecondary institutions, students, families, and community agencies can work together to enhance student success and educational attainment.

As this review demonstrates, we know many of the factors that facilitate and inhibit earning a bachelor's degree. To a lesser degree, we also know some of the more promising interventions that—if implemented effectively to reach large numbers of students—promise to increase this number. We certainly have much more to learn about these and related matters as demonstrated by the list of unanswered questions just presented.

Colleges and universities are limited in terms of what they can do to encourage student success. An institution of higher education cannot change the lineage of its students. Campus cultures do not change easily or willingly. Too many long-held beliefs and standard operating practices are tightly woven into an institution's ethos and embedded in the psyche of faculty leaders and senior administrators, some of which may be counterproductive. That said, most institutions can do far more than they are doing at present to implement interventions that will change the way students approach college and what they do after they arrive.

The real question is whether we have the *will* to more consistently use what we know to be promising policies and effective educational practices and thereby increase the odds that more students get ready, get in, and get through.

Appendix A: Note on Research Methods

We conducted this extensive literature review to develop an informed perspective on policies, programs, and practices that contribute to desired outcomes of postsecondary education. The research team developed a strategy for identifying relevant literature and created a list of key search terms, authors, and related topics to focus our work. More than seventy words, forty authors, and thirty organizations were identified as salient. In addition to searching for these terms using online library databases, we also devised a plan to explore reports found on pertinent foundations and organization Web sites. We consulted colleagues across the country to uncover additional research on student success that was less accessible through conventional means.

We then searched electronic library databases that house the vast majority of references on undergraduate student experiences, precollege characteristics, and institutional conditions that foster student success, including ERIC-EBSCO, a multidisciplinary, full-text database that contains references from more than thirty-one hundred scholarly publications; PsycINFO, which contains the international literature of psychology and related fields from more than thirteen hundred journals; and Sociological Abstracts, which contains the international literature in sociology and related disciplines in the social and behavioral sciences. We also examined relevant materials in the Indiana University Center for Postsecondary Research library and archives and findings from our ongoing survey work with several hundred colleges and universities nationwide.

These efforts yielded more than seven hundred relevant documents for our review. We were more inclusive with recent research articles and more selective with monographs, books, and articles that were fifteen years or older. We sorted these documents into four broad categories: precollege characteristics (two hundred relevant documents), postsecondary educational experiences (three hundred), institutional conditions (290), and postcollegiate outcomes (130). The total number of relevant books and articles in these four categories exceeded 700, as many articles pertained to more than one category. We divided up responsibility for reviewing the documents among the research team and created a database with full citations of articles.

The research team met face to face periodically to develop and fine-tune the search strategy, discuss our approach to reviewing the literature, share emerging findings and trends, identify deficiencies in documents collected, and discuss and revise the organization of the report. We developed a template to systematize our review of the literature so as to assess the value of the respective piece for answering the guiding research questions and to summarize key findings. After reviewing the majority of the literature, team members then wrote abstracts of key findings and insights from assigned categories of readings. These summaries were used to develop the major sections of the report. Drafts of sections were shared with the entire team. Finally, as the major sections of the report were completed, team members reviewed all segments and developed the recommendations and propositions.

Appendix B: Indicators of Student Success in Postsecondary Education

Student Goal Attainment: To what extent are students attaining their final educational goal as indicated on their application and advising records?

Course Retention and Success: At what rate do students complete the individual courses in which they enroll? At what rates are D, F, and W grades awarded in particular courses?

Success in Subsequent Coursework: How successful are students in courses that are linearly sequential, especially in math, science, and English?

Fall-to-Fall Persistence: At what rate do students continue their education from one complete academic year to the next in accordance with their educational goal?

Time to Degree: How many semesters elapse before degree attainment? What percentage of full-time students attempt and complete the average credit hour load per term?

Degree or Certificate Completion: What number and percentage of students complete their chosen degree or certificate program?

Graduate School Enrollment and Employment: At what level are students enrolling in graduate and professional school and attaining employment and advancement relevant to their degree or certificate program?

Transfer Rate and Success: At two-year institutions, what percentage of students complete their educational goal of transferring to a four-year institution? How does the success of transfer students compare with students who started at the institution?

Employer Assessment of Students: How satisfied are employers with students' knowledge, qualities, and skills?

Academic Value Added: What knowledge and skills have students acquired during their undergraduate experience?

Student Satisfaction: How satisfied are students with access, instructional and student services, facilities, and campus life?

Student Professional Growth and Development: What is the self-perceived personal growth, community involvement, and moral development of students completing their education at the institution?

Student Involvement: To what extent are students participating in educationally purposeful activities?

Citizenship and Engagement: To what extent are students acquiring habits of the mind and heart in college that will benefit them and society in the future?

Source: Adapted from American Association of Community Colleges, 1994; Harris, 1998.

References

Abraham, J. P., Lujan, S. S., Lopez, E. E., and Walker, M. T. (2002). Graduating students' perceptions of outcomes of college experiences at a predominantly Hispanic university. *Journal of Hispanic Higher Education, 1*(3), 267–276.

Achieve, Inc. (2006, February). *Closing the expectations gap 2006: An annual 50-state progress report on the alignment of high school policies with the demands of college and work.* Washington, DC: Achieve, Inc.

Adelman, C. (1999). *Answers in the toolbox: Academic intensity, attendance patterns, and bachelor's degree attainment.* Washington, DC: Office of Educational Research and Improvement, U.S. Department of Education.

Adelman, C. (2004) *Principal indicators of student academic histories in postsecondary education, 1972–2000.* Washington, DC: Institute of Education Sciences, U.S. Department of Education.

Adelman, C. (2005). Educational "anticipations" of traditional age community college students: A prolegomena to any future accountability indicators. *Journal of Applied Research in the Community College, 12*(1), 93–107.

Adelman, C. (2006a). *The propaganda of numbers in higher education.* Paper presented at the annual meeting of the American Educational Research Association, April, San Francisco, CA.

Adelman, C. (2006b). *The toolbox revisited: Paths to degree completion from high school through college.* Washington, DC: Office of Vocational and Adult Education, U.S. Department of Education.

Aitken, N. D. (1982). College student performance, satisfaction, and retention: Specification and estimation of structural equation model. *Journal of Higher Education, 53*(1), 32–50.

Aleman, A. (1994). *The cognitive value of college women's friendships.* Paper presented at the annual meeting of the American Educational Research Association, April, New Orleans, LA.

Alexander, L. T., Gur, R., and Patterson, L. (1974). Peer-assisted learning. *Improving Human Performance, 3*(4), 175–186.

Alexander, P. A., and Murphy, P. K. (1994). *The research base for APA's learner-centered psychological principles.* Paper presented at the annual meeting of the American Educational Research Association, April, New Orleans, LA.

Allen, C., Brower, A., and Golde, C. (1999). Wiser women: Fostering undergraduate success in science and engineering with a residential academic program. *Journal of Women and Minorities in Science and Engineering, 5*(3), 265–277.

Allen, D., and Duch, B. (1998). *Thinking toward solutions: Problem-based learning activities for general biology.* Fort Worth, TX: Harcourt College Publishing.

Allen, W. R. (1985). Black student, white campus: Structural, interpersonal, and psychological correlates of success. *Journal of Negro Education, 54*(2), 134–147.

Allen, W. R. (1992). The color of success: African-American college student outcomes at predominately white and historically black public colleges and universities. *Harvard Educational Review, 62*(1), 26–44.

Alpern, B. E. (2000). *Factors that influence community college transfer students' satisfaction with their baccalaureate institutions.* Troy, MI: Walsh College.

Amelink, C. T. (2005). *Predicting academic success among first-year, first generation students.* Unpublished doctoral dissertation, Virginia Polytechnic Institute and State University.

American Association of Community Colleges. (1994). *Community colleges: Core indicators of effectiveness.* AAC Special Reports No. 4. Washington, DC: American Association of Community Colleges.

American Association for Higher Education. (1992). *Assessment principles of good practices.* Washington, DC: American Association for Higher Education.

American College Testing Program. (2006). *Reading between the lines: What the ACT reading test reveals about college readiness.* Iowa City: American College Testing Program.

American Council on Education and American Association of University Professors. (2000). *Does diversity make a difference? Three research studies on diversity in college classrooms.* Executive Summary. Washington, DC: American Council on Education and American Association of University Professors.

American Diploma Project. (2004). *Ready or not: Creating a high school diploma that counts.* Executive Summary. Washington, DC: Achieve, Inc.

American Indian Higher Education Consortium, Institute for Higher Education Policy, and Sallie Mae Education Institute. (2000, May). *Creating role models for change: A survey of tribal college graduates.* Alexandria, VA: American Indian Higher Education Consortium, Institute for Higher Education Policy, and Sallie Mae Education Institute.

Anaya, G. (1996). College experiences and student learning: The influence of active learning, college environments, and co-curricular activities. *Journal of College Student Development, 37*(6), 611–622.

Angelo, T. A., and Cross, P. K. (1993). *Classroom assessment techniques: A Handbook for college teachers* (2nd ed.). San Francisco: Jossey-Bass.

Annis, L. F. (1983). The processes and effects of peer tutoring. *Human Learning: Journal of Practical Research & Applications, 2*(1), 39–47.

Anzaldua, G. (1987). *Borderlands = la frontera: The new mestiza.* San Francisco: Spinsters/Aunt Lute.

Association of American Colleges and Universities. (2002). *Greater expectations: A new vision for learning as a nation goes to college.* Washington, DC: Association of American Colleges and Universities.

Association of American Colleges and Universities. (2005). *Liberal education outcomes: A preliminary report on student achievement in college.* Washington, DC: Association of American Colleges and Universities.

Association of American Colleges and Universities. (2007). *College learning for the new global century.* Washington, DC: Association of American Colleges and Universities.

Astin, A. W. (1975). *The power of protest: A national study of student and faculty disruptions with implications for the future.* San Francisco: Jossey-Bass.

Astin, A. W. (1977). *Four critical years: Effects of college on beliefs, attitudes, and knowledge.* San Francisco: Jossey-Bass.

Astin, A. W. (1984). Student involvement: A developmental theory for higher education. *Journal of College Student Development, 25*(4), 297–308.

Astin, A. (1985a). *Achieving educational excellence.* San Francisco: Jossey-Bass.

Astin, A. W. (1985b). Involvement: The cornerstone of Excellence. *Change, 17*(4), 35–39.

Astin, A. W. (1991). The changing American college student: Implications for educational policy and practice. *Higher Education, 22*(2), 129–143.

Astin, A. W. (1993a). What matters in college. *Liberal Education, 79*(4), 4–15.

Astin, A. W. (1993b). *What matters in college? Four critical years revisited.* San Francisco: Jossey-Bass.

Astin, A. W., Tsui, L., and Avalos, J. (1996). *Degree attainment rates at American colleges and universities: Effects of race, gender, and institutional type* (No. HE 029 589). Los Angeles: Higher Education Research Institute, University of California.

Attinasi, L. C., Jr. (1989). Getting in: Mexican Americans' perceptions of university attendance and the implications for freshman year persistence. *Journal of Higher Education, 60*(3), 247–277.

Attinasi, L. C., Jr. (1992). Rethinking the study of the outcomes of college attendance. *Journal of College Student Development, 33*(1), 61–70.

Bailey, T., and Alfonso, M. (2005). *Paths to persistence: An analysis of research on program effectiveness at community colleges.* New Agenda Series, 6(1). Indianapolis: Lumina Foundation for Education.

Bailey, T., Badway, N., and Gumport, P. (2001). *For-profit higher education and community colleges.* Paper prepared for the National Center for Postsecondary Improvement (Deliverable #0400). Stanford, CA: Stanford University.

Bailey, T., Jenkins, D., and Leinbach, T. (2005). *Graduation rates, student goals, and measuring community college effectiveness* (CCRC Brief No. 28). New York: Community College Research Center, Columbia University.

Bailey, T., and others. (2005). *Beyond student right-to-know data: Factors that can explain community college graduation rates* (CCRC Brief No. 29). New York: Community College Research Center, Columbia University.

Baker, R. W., McNeil, O. V., and Siryk, B. (1985). Expectation and reality in freshman adjustment to college. *Journal of Counseling Psychology, 32*(1), 94–103.

Bandura, A. (1982). Self-efficacy mechanism in human agency. *American Psychologist, 37*(2), 122–147.

Bank, B., Slavings, R., and Biddle, R. (1990). Effects of peer, faculty, and parental influences on students' persistence. *Sociology of Education, 63*(3), 209–225.

Banning, J. H., and Bartels, S. (1997). A taxonomy: Campus physical artifacts as communicators of campus multiculturalism. *NASPA Journal, 35*(1), 29–37.

Banning, J. H., and Cunard, M. (1996). *Assessment and redesign of the physical environment in support of student development* (ACU-I Classics: Student Development). Bloomington, IN: ACU-I.

Bargh, J., and Schul, Y. (1980). On the cognitive benefits of teaching. *Journal of Educational Psychology, 72*(5), 593–604.

Barovick, H., and Baron, M. (2001, September 10). Indiana University: A web of friendly interest groups makes this big research institution feel less intimidating. *Time.* Retrieved January 2, 2006, from http://www.time.com/time/archive/preview/0,10987,1000722,00.html.

Barr, R. B., and Tagg, J. (1995). From teaching to learning: A new paradigm for undergraduate education. *Change, 27*(6), 12–25.

Baum, S., and Payea, K. (2004). Education pays 2004: The benefits of higher education for individual and society. New York: College Board.

Bauman, G. L., and others. (2005). *Achieving equitable educational outcomes with all students: The institution's roles and responsibilities.* Washington, DC: Association of American Colleges and Universities.

Baxter Magolda, M. B. (2001). *Making their own way: Narratives for transforming higher education to promote self-development.* Sterling, VA: Stylus.

Baxter Magolda, M. B. (2004). Self-authorship as the common goal of 21st-century education. In M. B. Baxter Magolda and P. M. King (Eds.), *Learning partnerships: Theory and models of practice to educate for self-authorship* (pp. 1–36). Sterling, VA: Stylus.

Bean, J. P. (1980). Dropouts and turnover: The synthesis and test of a causal model of student attrition. *Research in Higher Education, 12*(2), 155–187.

Bean, J. P. (1983). The application of a model of turnover in work organizations to the student attrition process. *Review of Higher Education, 6*(2), 129–148.

Bean, J. P. (1985). Interaction effects based on class level in an exploratory model of college student dropout syndrome. *American Educational Research Journal, 22*(1), 35–64.

Bean, J. P., and Bradley, R. (1986). Untangling the satisfaction-performance relationship for college students. *Journal of Higher Education, 57*(4), 393–412.

Bean, J. P., and Eaton, S. (2000). A psychological model of college student retention. In J. M. Braxton (Ed.), *Reworking the departure puzzle: New theory and research on college student retention* (pp. 73–89). Nashville: University of Vanderbilt Press.

Bean, J. P., and Kuh, G. D. (1984). The reciprocity between student-faculty informal contact and the academic performance of university students. *Research in Higher Education, 21*(4), 461–477.

Bean, J. P., and Vesper, N. (1994). *Gender differences in college student satisfaction.* Paper presented at the annual meeting of the Association for the Study of Higher Education, November, Tucson, AZ.

Becker, G. S. (1964). *Human capital: A theoretical and empirical analysis.* New York: Columbia University Press.

Becker, W. E., and Andrews, M. L. (Eds.). (2004). *The scholarship of teaching and learning in higher education: Contributions of research universities.* Bloomington: Indiana University Press.

Benitez, M. (1998). Hispanic-serving institutions: Challenges and opportunities. *New Directions for Higher Education, 26*(2), 57–68.

Bensimon, E. M. (2004). The diversity scorecard: A learning approach to institutional change. *Change, 36*(1), 44–53.

Benware, C., and Deci, E. (1984). Quality of learning with an active versus passive motivational set. *American Educational Research Journal, 21*(4), 755–765.

Berdie, R. F. (1966). College expectations, experiences, and perceptions. *Journal of College Student Personnel, 7,* 336–344.

Berdie, R. F. (1968). Changes in university perceptions during the first two years. *Journal of College Student Personnel, 9,* 85–89.

Berger, J. B. (2000). Optimizing capital, social reproduction, and undergraduate persistence. In J. M. Braxton (Ed.), *Reworking the student departure puzzle* (pp. 95–124). Nashville: Vanderbilt University Press.

Berger, J. B. (2002). The influence of the organizational structures of colleges and universities on college student learning. *Peabody Journal of Education, 77*(3), 40–59.

Berger, J. B., and Braxton, J. M. (1998). Revising Tinto's interactionalist theory of student departure through theory elaboration: Examining the role of organizational attributes in the persistence process. *Research in Higher Education, 39*(2), 103–119.

Berger, J. B., and Malaney, G. D. (2003). Assessing the transition of transfer students from community colleges to a university. *NASPA Journal, 40*(4). Retrieved December 1, 2005, from http://vnweb.hwwilsonweb.com/hww/shared/shared_main.jhtml;jsessionid= GAGWNWEN3WCI3QA3DINCFGGADUNGIIV0?_requestid=66495.

Berger, J. B., and Milem, J. F. (1999). The role of student involvement and perceptions of integration in a causal model of student persistence. *Research in Higher Education, 40*(6), 641–664.

Berger, J. B., and Milem, J. F. (2000). Organizational behavior in higher education and student outcomes. In J. C. Smart (Ed.), *Higher education: Handbook of theory and research* (Vol. 15, pp. 268–338). New York: Agathon.

Berkner, L., and Chavez, L. (1997). *Access to postsecondary education for the 1992 high school graduates.* (NCES 98–105). Washington, DC: National Center for Education Statistics, U.S. Department of Education.

Berkner, L., Cuccaro-Alamin, S., and McCormick, A. (1996). *Descriptive summary of 1989–90 beginning postsecondary students: Five years later.* (NCES 96–155). Washington, DC: National Center for Education Statistics, U.S. Department of Education.

Berliner, D. C. (1984). The half-full glass: A review of research on teaching. In P. L. Hosford (Ed.), *Using what we know about teaching* (pp. 51–84). Alexandria, VA: Association for Supervision and Curriculum Development.

Bettinger, E. P., and Long, B. T. (2005, May). *Addressing the needs of under-prepared students in higher education: Does college remediation work?* (NBER Working Paper 11325). Cambridge, MA: National Bureau of Economic Research.

Billson, J. M., and Terry, B. T. (1982). In search of the silken purse: Factors in attrition among first-generation students. *College and University, 58*(1), 57–75.

Birnbaum, R. (1988). How colleges work: The cybernetics of academic organization and leadership. San Francisco: Jossey-Bass.

Birnbaum, R. (1991). *Faculty in governance: The role of senates and joint committees in academic decision making.* San Francisco: Jossey-Bass.

Bishop, J. H. (2002). *What should be the federal role in supporting and shaping development of state accountability systems for secondary school achievement?* Paper presented at the Preparing America's Future: The High School Symposium, April, Washington, DC.

Bishop, J. H. (2004). Money and motivation. *Education Next, 4*(1), 62–67.

Blimling, G. S. (1989). A meta-analysis of the influence of college residence halls on academic performance. *Journal of College Student Development, 30*(4), 298–308.

Blimling, G. S. (1993). The influence of college residence halls on students. In J. C. Smart (Ed.), *Higher education: Handbook of theory and research* (Vol. 9, pp. 248–307). New York: Agathon.

Blimling, G. S., and Whitt, E. J. (1999). Identifying the principles that guide student affairs practice. In G. S. Blimling and E. J. Whitt (Eds.), *Good practice in student affairs: Principles to foster student learning* (pp. 1–20). San Francisco: Jossey-Bass.

Bloom, D., and Sommo, C. (2005). Building learning communities: Early results from the opening doors demonstration at Kingsborough community college. New York: Manpower Demonstration Research Corporation.

Blose, G. (1999). Modeled retention and graduation rates: Calculating expected retention and graduation rates for multicampus university systems. *New Directions for Higher Education, 27*(4), 69–86.

Bolman, L. G., and Deal, T. E. (1991). *Reframing organizations: Artistry, choice, and leadership.* San Francisco: Jossey-Bass.

Borden, V.M.H. (2004). Accommodating student swirl: When traditional students are no longer the tradition. *Change, 36*(2), 10–17.

Bourdieu, P., and Passeron, J. C. (1977). *Reproduction in education, society, and culture.* London: Sage.

Bourner, T. (1997). Teaching methods for learning outcomes. *Education + Training, 39*(9), 344–348.

Bowen, H. (1978). Some reflection on the current position and future outlook of American higher education. *Academe: Bulletin of the AAUP, 66*(1), 8–15.

Bowen, W. G., and Bok, D. C. (1998). The shape of the river: Long-term consequences of considering race in college and university admissions. Princeton, NJ: Princeton University Press.

Bowen, W. G., and Levin, S. A. (2003). *Reclaiming the game: College sports and educational values.* Princeton, NJ: Princeton University Press.

Boyer, E. L., and Hechinger, F. M. (1981). *Higher learning in the nation's service: A Carnegie Foundation essay.* Princeton, NJ: Carnegie Foundation for the Advancement of Teaching.

Boyer, P. (1995). Sharing power. *Tribal College Journal, 6*(4), 6–7.

Boyland, H. R. (2002) *What works: A guide to research-based best practices in developmental education.* Boone, NC: Continuous Quality Improvement Network with the National Center for Developmental Education, Appalachian State University.

Bradburn, E. M., and Hurst, D. G. (2001). Community college transfer rates to four-year institutions: Using alternative definitions of transfer. *Education Statistics Quarterly, 3*(3), 119–125.

Braswell, J. S., and others. (2001). *The nation's report card: Mathematics 2000.* Washington, DC: National Center for Education Statistics, U.S. Department of Education.

Braxton, J. M. (2000). Introduction: Reworking the student departure puzzle. In J. M. Braxton (Ed.), *Reworking the student departure puzzle* (pp. 1–8). Nashville, TN: Vanderbilt University Press.

Braxton, J. M. (2003). Student success. In S. R. Komives and D. B. Woodard, Jr. (Eds.), *Student services: A handbook for the profession* (4th ed., pp. 317–338). San Francisco: Jossey-Bass.

Braxton, J. M., Hirschy, A. S., and McClendon, S. A. (2004). *Understanding and reducing college student departure.* ASHE-ERIC Higher Education Report, Vol. 30, No. 3. Washington, DC: School of Education and Human Development, The George Washington University.

Braxton, J. M., and McClendon, S. A. (2001–02). The fostering of social integration and retention through institutional practice. *Journal of College Student Retention: Research, Theory and Practice, 3*(1), 57–71.

Braxton, J. M., Milem, J. F., and Sullivan, A. S. (2000). The influence of active learning on the college student departure process: Toward a revision of Tinto's theory. *Journal of Higher Education, 71*(5), 569–590.

Braxton, J. M., Sullivan, A., S., and Johnson, R. T. (1997). Appraising Tinto's theory of college student departure. In J. C. Smart (Ed.), *Higher education: Handbook of theory and research* (Vol. 12, pp. 107–158). New York: Agathon.

Braxton, J. M., Vesper, N., and Hossler, D. (1995). Expectations for college and student persistence. *Research in Higher Education, 36*(5), 595–612.

Breland, H., and others. (2002, March). Trends in college admission 2000: A report of a national survey of undergraduate admission policies, practices, and procedures. Alexandria, VA: National Association for College Admission Counseling.

Bridges, B. K., Kinzie, J., Nelson Laird, T. F., and Kuh, G. D. (forthcoming). Student engagement and student success at minority serving institutions. In M. Gasman, B. Baez, and C.S.V. Turner (Eds.), *Interdisciplinary approaches to understanding minority institutions.* Albany: SUNY Press.

Bridglall, B. L., and Gordon, E. W. (2002). The idea of supplementary education. *Pedagogical Inquiry and Praxis* (No. 3). New York: Teachers College, Columbia University, Institute for Urban and Minority Education.

Brigman, S., Kuh, G. D., and Stager, S. (1982). Those who choose to leave: Why students voluntarily withdraw from college. *Journal of the National Association of Women Deans, Administrators, and Counselors, 45*(3), 3–8.

Burley, A., Cejda, B., and Butner, B. (2001). Dropout and stopout patterns among developmental education students in Texas community colleges. *Community College Journal of Research and Practice, 25*(10), 767–782.

Cabrera, A. F., Casteneda, M. B., Nora, A., and Hengstler, D. (1992). The convergence between two theories of college persistence. *Journal of Higher Education, 63*(2), 143–164.

Cambridge, B. L. (1996). The paradigm shifts: Examining quality of teaching through assessment of student learning. *Innovative Higher Education, 20*(4), 287–297.

Camera, W. J. (2003, March). *College persistence, graduation, and remediation.* College Board Research Notes No. 19. Retrieved April 1, 2006, from http://search.collegeboard.com/research/pdf/rn19_22643.pdf.

Cantor, N., and Mischel, W. (1977). Traits and prototypes: Effects of recognition memory. *Journal of Personality and Social Psychology, 35*(1), 38–49.

Carey, K. (2004, May). A matter of degrees: Improving graduation rates in four-year colleges and universities. Washington, DC: Education Trust.

Carini, R. M., Kuh, G. D., and Klein, S. P. (2006). Student engagement and student learning: Testing the linkages. *Research in Higher Education, 47*(1), 1–32.

Carnevale, A. P., and Desrochers, D. M. (2003). Preparing students for the knowledge economy: What school counselors need to know. *Professional School Counseling, 6*(4), 228–236.

Carroll, D. (1989). *College persistence and degree attainment for the 1980 high school graduates: Hazards for transfers, stopouts, and part-timers.* (NCES 89–302). Washington, DC: National Center for Education Statistics, U.S. Department of Education.

Carroll, J. (1988). Freshman retention and attrition factors at a predominately black urban community college. *Journal of College Student Development, 29*(1), 52–59.

Carstens, J. B. (2000). *Effects of a freshman orientation course on academic outcomes, quality of effort and estimated intellectual gain.* Doctoral dissertation, University of Iowa. *Dissertation Abstracts International, 61,* 2206.

Carter, D. F. (1999). The impact of institutional choice and environments on African-American and white students' degree expectations. *Research in Higher Education, 40*(1), 17–41.

Carter, D. J., and Wilson, R. (1997). *Minorities in higher education: 1996–1997 Fifteenth annual status report.* Washington, DC: Office of Minority Concerns, American Council on Education.

Cashin, W. E. (1988). *Student ratings of teaching: A summary of the research* (IDEA Paper No. 20). Manhattan, KS: Kansas State University, Center for Faculty Evaluation and Development, Division of Continuing Education.

Cejda, B. D., and Kaylor, A. J. (2001). Early transfer: A case study of traditional-aged community college students. *Community College Journal of Research and Practice, 25*(8), 621–638.

Chamberlain, T. A. (2005). *Branching out or breaking off: An exploration of first-year students' social network.* Unpublished manuscript. Bloomington: Indiana University.

Chang, M. J. (1999). Does racial diversity matter? The educational impact of a racially diverse undergraduate population. *Journal of College Student Development, 40*(4), 377–395.

Chang, M. J. (2000). *Is it more than about getting along? The broader educational implications of reducing students' racial biases.* Paper presented at the annual meeting of the Association for the Study of Higher Education, November, San Antonio, TX.

Chen, X. (2005). *First generation students in postsecondary education: A look at their college transcripts.* (NCES 2005–171). Washington, DC: U.S. Government Printing Office.

Chickering, A. W. (2006). Creating conditions so every student can learn. *About Campus, 11*(2), 9–15.

Chickering, A. W., and Gamson, Z. F. (Eds.). (1987). Seven principles for good practice in undergraduate education. *AAHE Bulletin, March,* 3–7.

Chickering, A. W., and Gamson, Z. F. (1991). Applying the seven principles for good practice in undergraduate education. San Francisco: Jossey-Bass.

Chickering, A. W., and Reisser, L. (1993). *Education and identity* (2nd ed.). San Francisco: Jossey-Bass.

Choy, S. P. (1999). College access and affordability. *Education Statistics Quarterly, 1*(2), 74–90.

Choy, S. P. (2001). *Students whose parents did not go to college: Postsecondary access, persistence, and attainment.* (NCES 2001–126). Washington, DC: National Center for Education Statistics, U.S. Department of Education.

Chrispeels, J. H., and Rivero, E. (2001). Engaging Latino families for student success: How parent education can reshape parents' sense of place in the education of their children. *Peabody Journal of Education, 76*(2), 119–169.

Christie, N., and Dinham, S. (1991). Institutional and external influences on social integration in the freshman year. *Journal of Higher Education, 62*(4), 412–436.

Cohen, A. M. (1996). Orderly thinking about a chaotic system. *New Directions for Community Colleges, 24*(4), 25–34.

Cohen, A. M., and Brawer, F. (1987). *The collegiate function of community colleges.* San Francisco: Jossey-Bass.

Cohen, A. M., and Brawer, F. B. (1996). *Policies and programs that affect transfer.* Washington, DC: American Council on Education.

Coleman, H. L., and Freeman, A. M. (1996). Effects of a structured group intervention on the achievement of academically at-risk undergraduates. *Journal of College Student Development, 37*(6), 631–636.

Coleman, J. S. (1988). Social capital in the creation of human capital. *American Journal of Sociology, 94,* 95–120.

Collins, J. C. (2001). *Good to great: Why some companies make the leap—and others don't.* New York: Harper Business.

Committee for Economic Development. (2005). Cracks in the education pipeline: A business leader's guide to higher education reform. Washington, DC: Committee for Economic Development.

Community College Survey of Student Engagement. (2004). *Engagement by design: 2004 findings.* Austin, TX: Community College Survey of Student Engagement.

Community College Survey of Student Engagement. (2005). *Engaging students, challenging the odds: 2005 findings.* Austin, TX: Community College Survey of Student Engagement.

Conley, D. T. (2003). Connecting the dots: Linking high schools and postsecondary education to increase student success. *Peer Review, 5*(2), 9–12.

Conyne, R. K., and Clack, R. J. (1981). *Environmental assessment and design: A new tool for the applied behavioral scientist.* New York: Praeger.

Cook, B., and King, J. E. (2005). *Improving lives through higher education: Campus programs and policies for low-income adults.* Washington, DC: Lumina Foundation for Education and American Council on Education Center for Policy Analysis.

Cross, K. P. (1987). *Teaching "for" learning.* Paper presented at the North Carolina State University Centennial Year Provost's Forum, February, Raleigh, NC.

Cross, K. P. (1998). Classroom research: Implementing the scholarship of teaching. *New Directions for Teaching and Learning, 75,* 5–12.

Cross, K. P. (1999). What do we know about students' learning, and how do we know it? *Innovative Higher Education, 23*(4), 255–270.

Crosson, P. H. (1988). Four-year college and university environments for minority degree achievement. *Review of Higher Education, 11*(4), 365–382.

Cruce, T., Wolniak, G. C., Seifert, T. A., and Pascarella, E. T. (2006). Impacts of good practices on cognitive development, learning orientations, and graduate degree plans during the first year of college. *Journal of College Student Development, 47,* 365–383.

Cuseo, J. B. (1998). *The transfer transition: A summary of key issues, target areas, and tactics for reform.* (ED 425–771)

Dawson-Threat, J. (1997). Enhancing in-class academic experiences for African American men. *New Directions for Student Services, 80,* 31–41.

Dayton, B., Gonzalez-Vasquez, N., Martinez, C. R., and Plum, C. (2004). Hispanic-serving institutions through the eyes of students and administrators. In A. M. Ortiz (Ed.), *Addressing the unique needs of Latino American students,* New Directions for Student Services (Vol. 105, pp. 29–39). San Francisco: Jossey-Bass.

de los Santos, A., Jr., and Wright, I. (1990). Maricopa's swirling students: Earning one-third of Arizona State's bachelor's degrees. *Community, Technical, and Junior College Journal, 60*(6), 32–34.

Dougherty, K. J. (1994). *The contradictory college: The conflicting origins, impacts, and futures of the community college.* Albany: State University of New York Press.

Duch, B. J., Gron, S. E., and Allen, D. E. (Eds.). (2001). *The power of problem-based learning: A practical "how to" for teaching undergraduate courses in any discipline.* Sterling, VA: Stylus Publishing.

Dunphy, L., Miller, T., Woodruff, T., and Nelson, J. (1987). Exemplary retention strategies for the freshman year. *New Directions in Higher Education, 15*(4), 39–60.

Dweck, C. S. (2000). *Self-theories: Their role in motivation, personality, and development.* Philadelphia: Psychology Press.

Dweck, C. S., and Leggett, E. L. (1988). A social-cognitive approach to motivation and personality. *Psychological Review, 95*(2), 256–273.

Ebert-May, D., Brewer, C., and Allred, S. (1997). Innovation in large lectures—teaching for active learning. *Bioscience, 47*(9), 601–607.

Education Commission of the States. (1995). *Making quality count in undergraduate education.* Denver: ECS Distribution Center.

Ehrenberg, R. G., and Rothstein, D. S. (1994). Do historically black institutions of higher education confer unique advantages on black students? An initial analysis. In R. G. Ehrenberg (Ed.), *Choices and consequences: Contemporary policy issues in education* (pp. 89–137). Ithaca, NY: ILR Press.

Eimers, M. T., and Pike, G. R. (1997). Minority and nonminority adjustment to college: Differences or similarities? *Research in Higher Education, 38*(1), 77–97.

Ethington, C. A., and Smart, J. C. (1986). Persistence to graduate education. *Research in Higher Education, 24*(3), 287–303.

Ewell, P. T. (1989). Institutional characteristics and faculty/administrator perceptions of outcomes: An exploratory analysis. *Research in Higher Education, 30*(2), 113–136.

Fallows, J., Bakke, D., Ganeshananthan, V. V., and Johnson, C. (2003, November). The new college chaos. *Atlantic Monthly, 292*(4), 106–114.

Feagin, J. R., Vera, H., and Imani, N. (1996). *The agony of education: Black students at white colleges and universities.* New York: Routledge.

Feldman, D. C. (1981). The multiple socialization of organizational members. *Academy of Management Review, 6*(2), 308–318.

Feldman, K. A. (1976). The superior college teacher from the students' view. *Research in Higher Education, 5*(3), 243–288.

Feldman, K. A., and Newcomb, T. M. (1969). *The impact of college on students.* San Francisco: Jossey-Bass.

Fidler, P. P., and Hunter, M. (1989). How seminars enhance student success. In M. Upcraft, J. Gardner, and Associates (Eds.), *The freshman year experience: Helping students survive and succeed in college* (pp. 216–237). San Francisco: Jossey-Bass.

Finn, C. E., Jr. (2006, March 10). Obstacles on the route from high school to college. *Chronicle of Higher Education,* B40.

Finney, J. E., and Kelly, P. J. (2004). Affordability: Obtaining and making sense of information about how students, families, and states pay for higher education. *Change, 36*(4), 54–60.

Fischer, N. M. (1995). *The long-term effects of undergraduate student involvement experiences on selected outcome measures.* Paper presented at the annual meeting of the Association for Institutional Research, May, Boston, MA.

Fitzgerald, B. K. (2004). Missed opportunities: Has college opportunity fallen victim to policy drift? *Change, 36*(4), 10–20.

Florida Department of Education. (2005, March). *Postsecondary success begins with high school preparation.* Data Trend #33. Tallahassee: Florida Department of Education.

Forest, A. (1985). Creating conditions for student and institutional success. In L. Noel, R. S. Levitz, D. Saluri, and Associates (Eds.), *Increasing student retention: Effective programs and practices for reducing dropout rate.* San Francisco: Jossey-Bass.

Fries-Britt, S., and Turner, B. (2002). Uneven stories: Successful black collegians at a black and a white campus. *Review of Higher Education, 25*(3), 315–330.

Frost, S. (2003). The shortchanged high school. *American School Board Journal, 190*(1), 29–31.

Ganderton, P., and Santos, R. (1995). Hispanic college attendance and completion: Evidence from the High School and Beyond surveys. *Economics of Education Review, 14*(1), 35–46.

Garcia, P. (2001). *Understanding obstacles and barriers to Hispanic baccalaureates.* Arlington, VA: RAND Corporation. (ED 477 485).

Gardner, J. N., and Jewler, A. J. (1995). *Your college experience: Strategies for success* (2nd ed.). Boston: Wadsworth-Thomson.

General Accounting Office. (1995). *Higher education: Restructuring student aid could reduce low-income student dropout rate* (GAO/HEHS-95-48). Washington, DC: U.S. Government Printing Office.

Gerken, J. T., and Volkwein, J. F. (2000). *Precollege characteristics and freshman year experiences as predictors of eight-year college outcomes.* Paper presented at the annual meeting of the Association for Institutional Research, May, Cincinnati, OH.

Gladieux, L. E., and Swail, W. S. (1998). Financial aid is not enough: Improving the odds of college success. *College Board Review, 185,* 16–21.

Gleason, P. (1993). College student employment, academic progress, and postcollege labor market success. *Journal of Student Financial Aid, 23*(2), 5–14.

Godwin, G. J., and Markham, W. T. (1996). First encounters of the bureaucratic kind: Early freshman experiences with a campus bureaucracy. *Journal of Higher Education, 67*(6), 660–691.

Goldin, C., Katz, L. F., and Kuziemko, I. (2006, March). *The homecoming of American college women: The reversal of the college gender gap* (NBER Working Paper 12139). Cambridge, MA: National Bureau of Economic Research.

Goldschmid, B., and Goldschmid, M. (1976). Peer teaching in higher education: A review. *Higher Education, 4*(1), 9–33.

Gonyea, R. M. (2005). *The relationship between student engagement and selected desirable undergraduate outcomes in the first year of college.* Unpublished doctoral dissertation, Indiana University Bloomington.

Gonzales, J. L., Jr. (1996). *Discrimination and conflict: Minority status and the Latino community in the United States.* Davis: University of California, Davis. (ED 413 158)

Gonzalez, J. M., and Szecsy, E. M. (2002). *The condition of Hispanic education in Arizona, 2002.* Tempe: Arizona State University.

Gonzalez, K. P. (2000–01). Toward a theory of minority student participation in predominantly white colleges and universities. *Journal of College Student Retention, 2*(1), 69–91.

Gonzalez, N. A., Cauce, A. M., Friedman, R. J., and Mason, C. A. (1996). Family, peer, and neighborhood influences on academic achievement among African-American adolescents: One-year prospective effects. *American Journal of Community Psychology, 24*(3), 365–387.

Goodsell, A. S., Maher, M., and Tinto, V. (1992). *Collaborative learning: A sourcebook for higher education* (Vol. 1.). University Park, PA: National Center on Postsecondary Teaching, Learning, and Assessment.

Gordon, E. W. (1999). *Education and justice: A view from the back of the bus.* New York: Teachers College Press.

Graunke, S. S., and Woosley, S. A. (2005). An exploration of the factors that affect the academic success of college sophomores. *College Student Journal, 39*(2), 367–377.

Grubb, W. N. (2001, February). *From black box to Pandora's box: Evaluating remedial/developmental education.* New York: Community College Research Center, Teachers College, Columbia University.

Guerin, K. (1997). *Tracking student stop-out, transfer and graduation: An event history analysis of competing risks.* Paper presented at the annual meeting of the Association for Institutional Research, May, Orlando, FL.

Gumport, P. J. (2001). Built to serve: The enduring legacy of public higher education. In P. G. Altbach, P. J. Gumport, and D. B. Johnstone (Eds.), *In defense of American higher education* (pp. 85–109). Baltimore: Johns Hopkins University Press.

Gurin, P. (1999). The compelling need for diversity in higher education: *Gratz et al. v. Bollinger et al.* No. 97–75237 and *Grutter et al. v. Bollinger et al.* No. 97–75928. Ann Arbor: University of Michigan.

Gurin P., and Epps, E. (1975). Black consciousness, identity, and achievement: A study of students in historically black colleges. New York: Wiley.

Guskin, A. E. (1994). Reducing student costs and enhancing student learning: The university challenge of the 1990s. Part II: Restructuring the role of faculty. *Change, 26*(5), 16–25.

Guskin, A. E. (1997). Learning more, spending less. *About Campus, 2*(3), 4–9.

Gutierrez, R. (2000). Advancing African-American, urban youth in mathematics: Unpacking the success of one math department. *American Journal of Education, 109*(1), 63–111.

Hamrick, F. A., and Stage, F. K. (2004). College predisposition at high-minority enrollment, low-income schools. *Review of Higher Education, 27*(2), 151–168.

Hanks, M. P., and Eckland, B. K. (1976). Athletics and social participation in the education attainment process. *Sociology of Education, 49*(4), 271–294.

Hanniford, B., and Sagoria, M. (1994). *The impact of work family roles on associate and baccalaureate degree completion among students in early adulthood.* Paper presented at the annual meeting of the American Educational Research Association, April, New Orleans, LA.

Harker, R. K. (1984). On reproduction, habitus, and education. *British Journal of Sociology, 5*(2), 117–127.

Harvey, W. B. (2001). *Minorities in higher education 2000–2001: Eighteenth annual status report.* Washington, DC: American Council on Education.

Hassel, H., and Laurey, J. (2005). The dea(r)th of student responsibility. *College Teaching, 53*(1), 2–13.

Hayek, J. C., Carini, R. M., O'Day, P. T., and Kuh, G. D. (2002). Triumph or tragedy: Comparing student engagement levels of members of Greek-letter organizations and other students. *Journal of College Student Development, 43*(5), 643–663.

Hearn, J. C. (1987). Impacts of undergraduate experiences on aspirations and plans for graduate and professional education. *Research in Higher Education, 27*(2), 119–141.

Heath, T. (1992). *Predicting the educational aspiration and graduate plans of black and white college and university students: When do dreams become realities?* Paper presented at the annual meeting of the Association for the Study of Higher Education, October, Minneapolis, MN.

Hedlund, D., and Jones, J. (1970). Effects of student personnel services on completion rates in two-year colleges. *Journal of College Student Personnel, 11*(3), 196–199.

Heller, D. E. (2001). *Debts and decisions: Student loans and their relationship to graduate school and career choice.* New Agenda Series. Indianapolis: Lumina Foundation.

Heller, D. E. (Ed.). (2002). *Conditions of access: Higher education for lower-income students.* Westport, CT: American Council on Education/Praeger Series on Higher Education.

Heller, D. E. (2004). The changing nature of financial aid. *Academe, 90*(4), 36–38.

Helmcamp, A., and Petrie, T. A. (1998). Evaluation of an academic skills course. *Journal of College Student Development, 39*(1), 112–116.

Hernandez, J. C. (2000). Understanding the retention of Latino college students. *Journal of College Student Development, 41*(6), 575–588.

High School Survey of Student Engagement. (2005). *Getting students ready for college: What student engagement data can tell us.* Bloomington: Indiana University.

Himelhoch, C. R., Nichols, A., Ball, S. R., and Black, L. C. (1997). *A comparative study of the factors [that] predict persistence for African American students at historically black institutions and predominantly white institutions.* Paper presented at the annual meeting of the Association for the Study of Higher Education, November, Albuquerque, NM.

Hoachlander, G., Sikora, A. C., and Horn, L. (2003). *Community college students: Goals, academic preparation, and outcomes.* (NCES 2003–164). Washington, DC: National Center for Education Statistics, U.S. Department of Education.

Hoffman, K., Llagas, C., and Snyder, T. D. (2003). *Status and trends in the education of blacks.* (NCES 2003–034). Washington, DC: National Center for Education Statistics, U.S. Department of Education.

Hoffman, N. (2005, April). *Add and subtract: Dual enrollment as a state strategy to increase postsecondary success for underrepresented students.* Boston: Jobs for the Future.

Holland, A., and Huba, M. E. (1991). Satisfaction with college among participants in a campus service program. *NASPA Journal, 28*(4), 342–347.

Holland, J. L. (1973). *Making vocational choices: A theory of careers.* Englewood Cliffs, NJ: Prentice-Hall.

Horn, L. J. (1998). *Stopouts or stayouts? Undergraduates who leave college in their first year.* (NCES 1999–087). Washington, DC: National Center for Education Statistics, U.S. Department of Education.

Horn, L. J., and Berger, R. (2004). *College persistence on the rise? Changes in five-year degree completion and postsecondary persistence rates between 1994 and 2000.* (NCES 2005–156). Washington, DC: National Center for Education Statistics, U.S. Department of Education.

Horn, L. J., and Kojaku, L. K. (2001). High school academic curriculum and the persistence path through college: Persistence and transfer behavior of undergraduates three years after entering four-year institutions. *Education Statistics Quarterly, 3*(3), 65–72.

Horn, L. J., and Premo, M. (1995). *Profile of undergraduates in U.S. postsecondary institutions: 1992–93.* (NCES 96–237). Washington, DC: National Center for Education Statistics, U.S. Department of Education.

Hossler, D., Kuh, G. D., and Olsen, D. (2001). Finding fruit on the vines: Using higher educational research and institutional research to guide institutional policies and strategies. Part II. *Research in Higher Education, 42*(2), 223–235.

Hossler, D., and Schmit, J. (1995). The Indiana postsecondary-encouragement experiment. *New Directions for Higher Education, 89,* 27–39.

Hossler, D., Schmit, J., and Vesper, N. (1999). *Going to college: How social, economic, and educational factors influence the decisions students make.* Baltimore: Johns Hopkins University Press.

Howard, J. A. (2005). Why should we care about student expectations? In T. E. Miller, B. E. Bender, J. S. Schuh, and Associates (Eds.), *Promoting reasonable expectations: Aligning student and institutional views of the college experience* (pp. 10–33). San Francisco: Jossey-Bass.

Hoyt, J. E. (1999). Remedial education and student attrition. *Community College Review, 27*(2), 51–72.

Hu, S. (Ed.). (2005). *Beyond grade inflation: Grading problems in higher education.* ASHE Higher Education Report Vol. 30, No. 6. Washington, DC: School of Education and Human Development, The George Washington University.

Hu, S., and Kuh, G. D. (2002). Being (dis)engaged in educationally purposeful activities: The influences of student and institutional characteristics. *Research in Higher Education, 43*(5), 555–575.

Hu, S., and Kuh, G. D. (2003a). Diversity experiences and college student learning and personal development. *Journal of College Student Development, 44*(3), 320–334.

Hu, S., and Kuh, G. D. (2003b). Maximizing what students get out of college: Testing a learning productivity model. *Journal of College Student Development, 44*(2), 185–203.

Hughes, K. L., Karp, M. M., Fermin, B. J., and Bailey, T. R. (2005). *Pathways to college access and success.* Washington, DC: Office of Vocational and Adult Education, U.S. Department of Education.

Hughes, R., and Pace, C. R. (2003). Using NSSE to study student retention and withdrawal. *Assessment Update, 15*(4), 1–2.

Hurtado, S. (1994). The institutional climate for talented Latino students. *Research in Higher Education, 35*(1), 21–41.

Hurtado, S., and Carter, D. F. (1997). Effects of college transition and perceptions of the campus racial climate on Latino students' sense of belonging. *Sociology of Education, 70*(4), 324–345.

Hurtado, S., Carter, D. F., and Spuler, A. (1996). Latino student transition to college: Assessing difficulties and factors in successful college adjustment. *Research in Higher Education, 37*(2), 135–157.

Hurtado, S., Dey, E. L., Gurin, P. Y., and Gurin, G. (2003). College environments, diversity, and student learning. In J. C. Smart (Ed.), *Higher education: Handbook of theory and research* (Vol. 13, pp. 145–189). Boston: Kluwer Academic Publishers.

Hurtado, S., Milem, J. F., Clayton-Pedersen, A. R., and Allen, W. R. (1998). Enhancing campus climates for racial/ethnic diversity: Educational policy and practice. *Review of Higher Education, 21*(3), 279–302.

Hurtado, S., Milem, J. F., Clayton-Pedersen, A. R., and Allen, W. R. (1999). *Enacting diverse learning environments: Improving the climate for racial/ethnic diversity in higher education.* ASHE-ERIC Higher Education Report, Vol. 26, No. 8. Washington, DC: School of Education and Human Development, The George Washington University.

Hurtado, S., and Ponjuan, L. (2005). Latino educational outcomes and the campus climate. *Journal of Hispanic Higher Education, 4*(3), 235–251.

Hutchings, P. (1996). The peer review of teaching: progress, issues, and prospects. *Innovative Higher Education, 20*(4), 221–234.

Ignash, J. M. (1997). Who should provide postsecondary remedial/developmental education? *New Directions for Community Colleges, 100*, 5–9.

Illinois State Board of Higher Education. (2003). *Assessing progress toward meeting the goals of "The Illinois Commitment": Performance indicators.* 2003 Annual Report. Springfield: Illinois State Board of Higher Education.

Immerwahr, J. (2000). Great expectations: How the public and parents—white, African American, and Hispanic—view higher education. New York: Public Agenda Foundation.

Immerwahr, J. (2003). *With diploma in hand: Hispanic high school seniors talk about their futures.* New York: Public Agenda and National Center for Public Policy and Higher Education.

Institute for Higher Education Policy. (1995, June*). The next step: Student aid for student success.* Washington, DC: Institute for Higher Education Policy.

Institute for Higher Education Policy. (1998, December). *College remediation: What it is, what it costs, what's at stake.* Washington, DC: Institute for Higher Education Policy.

Institute for Higher Education Policy. (2001, February). *Getting through college: Voices of low-income and minority students in New England.* Washington, DC: Institute for Higher Education Policy.

Jalomo, R. (1995). *Latino students in transition: An analysis of the first-year experience in community college.* Unpublished doctoral dissertation, Arizona State University.

Johnstone, D. B. (2005). Fear and loathing of tuition fees: An American perspective on higher education finance in the UK. *Perspectives: Policy and Practice in Higher Education, 9*(1), 12–16.

Jones, C. E., and Watt, J. D. (1999). Psychosocial development and moral orientation among traditional-aged college students. *Journal of College Student Development, 40*(2), 125–132.

Juillerat, S. (2000). Assessing the expectations and satisfactions of sophomores. In L. A. Schreiner and J. Pattengale (Eds.), *Visible solutions for invisible students: Helping sophomores succeed* (Monograph 31, pp.19–29). Columbia, SC: National Resource Center for the First-Year Experience and Students in Transition, University of South Carolina.

Kappner, A. S. (2002). *Across the education continuum: Child care on the college campus.* Cedar Falls, IA: National Coalition for Campus Children's Centers.

Kenny, M. E., and Perez, V. (1996). Attachment and psychological well-being among racially and ethnically diverse first-year college students. *Journal of College Student Development, 37*(5), 527–535.

Kenny, M. E., and Stryker, S. (1996). Social network characteristics and college adjustment among racially and ethnically diverse first-year students. *Journal of College Student Development, 37*(6), 649–658.

Kezar, A., and Kinzie, J. (2006). Examining the ways institutions create student engagement: The role of mission. *Journal of College Student Development, 47*(2), 149–172.

Kim, M. M. (2002). Historically black vs. white institutions: Academic development among black students. *Review of Higher Education, 25*(4), 385–407.

King, J. E. (2000). *Gender equity in higher education: Are male students at a disadvantage?* Washington, DC: Center for Policy Analysis, American Council on Education.

Kinzie, J., and others. (2004). *Fifty years of college choice: Social, political and institutional influences on the decision-making process.* Indianapolis: Lumina Foundation for Education.

Kinzie, J., and others. (2007). Women students at coeducational and women's colleges: How do their experiences compare? *Journal of College Student Development, 48*(2).

Kirst, M. W., and Venezia, A. (2006, March 10). What states must do. *Chronicle of Higher Education,* B36.

Kleiner, B., and Lewis, L. (2005). *Dual enrollment of high school students at postsecondary institutions: 2002–03.* (NCES 2005–008). Washington, DC: National Center for Education Statistics, U.S. Department of Education.

Knapp, L. G., Kelly-Reid, J. E., and Whitmore, R. W. (2006). Enrollment in postsecondary institutions, fall 2004; graduation rates, 1998 and 2001 cohorts; and financial statistics, fiscal year 2004. (NCES 2006–155). Washington, DC: National Center for Education Statistics, U.S. Department of Education. Retrieved March 14, 2006, from http://nces.ed.gov/pubsearch/pubsinfo.asp?pubid=2006155.

Knight, W. E. (2003). Learning communities and first-year programs: Lessons for planners. *Planning for Higher Education, 31*(4), 5–12.

Kowalski, C. (1977). The impact of college on persisting and nonpersisting students. New York: Philosophical Library.

Kramer, G. L., and Associates (2003). *Student academic services: An integrated approach.* San Francisco: Jossey-Bass.

Kuh, G. D. (1993). In their own words: What students learn outside the classroom. *American Educational Research Journal, 30*(2), 277–304.

Kuh, G. D. (1995). The other curriculum: Out-of-class experiences associated with student learning and personal development. *Journal of Higher Education, 66*(2), 123–155.

Kuh, G. D. (1999). A framework for understanding student affairs work. *Journal of College Student Development, 40*(5), 530–537.

Kuh, G. D. (2000). Do environments matter? A comparative analysis of the impress of different types of colleges and universities on character. *Journal of College and Character.* Retrieved January 3, 2006, from http://collegevalues.org/articles.cfm?a=1andid=239.

Kuh, G. D. (2001). Assessing what really matters to student learning: Inside the national survey of student engagement. *Change, 33*(3), 10–17.

Kuh, G. D. (2003). What we're learning about student engagement from NSSE: Benchmarks for effective educational practices. *Change, 35*(2), 24–32.

Kuh, G. D. (2004). The contributions of the research university to assessment and innovation in undergraduate education. In W. E. Becker and M. L. Andrews (Eds.), *The scholarship of teaching and learning in higher education: The contributions of research universities* (pp. 81–98). Bloomington: Indiana University Press.

Kuh, G. D. (2005). Student engagement in the first year of college. In M. L. Upcraft, J. N. Gardner, and B. O. Barefoot (Eds.), *Challenging and supporting the first-year student: A handbook for improving the first year of college* (pp. 86–107). San Francisco: Jossey-Bass.

Kuh, G. D. (2006). Built to engage: Liberal arts colleges and effective educational practice. In F. Oakely (Ed.), *Liberal arts colleges in American higher education* (ACLS occasional paper) (pp. 122–150). New York: American Council of Learned Societies.

Kuh, G. D., Douglas, K. B., Lund, J. P., and Ramin-Gyurnek, J. (1994). *Student learning outside the classroom: Transcending artificial boundaries.* ASHE-ERIC Higher Education Report No. 8. Washington, DC: Graduate School of Education and Human Development, The George Washington University.

Kuh, G. D., Gonyea, R. M., and Williams, J. M. (2005). What students expect from college and what they get. In T. Miller, B. Bender, J. Schuh, and Associates (Eds.), *Promoting reasonable expectations: Aligning student and institutional thinking about the college experience* (pp. 34–64). San Francisco: Jossey-Bass and National Association of Student Personnel Administrators.

Kuh, G. D., and Hu, S. (1999). *Learning productivity at research universities.* Paper presented at the annual meeting of the American Educational Research Association, April, Montreal, Quebec.

Kuh, G. D., and Hu, S. (2001a). The effects of student-faculty interaction in the 1990s. *Review of Higher Education, 24*(3), 309–332.

Kuh, G. D., and Hu, S. (2001b). The relationships between computer and information technology use, selected learning and personal development outcomes, and other college experiences. *Journal of College Student Development, 42*(3), 217–232.

Kuh, G. D., Hu, S., and Vesper, N. (2000). "They shall be known by what they do": An activities-based typology of college students. *Journal of College Student Development, 41*(2), 228–244.

Kuh, G. D., Kinzie, J., Buckley, J., Bridges, B., & Hayek, J. C. (2006, November). *What matters to student success: A review of the literature.* Final report for the National Postsecondary Education Cooperative and National Center for Education Statistics. Bloomington: Indiana University Center for Postsecondary Research. Retrieved February 3, 2007, from http://nces.ed.gov/npec/pdf/Kuh_Team_Report.pdf.

Kuh, G. D., Kinzie, J., Schuh, J. H., and Whitt, E. J. (2005). *Assessing conditions to enhance educational effectiveness: The inventory for student engagement and success.* San Francisco: Jossey-Bass.

Kuh, G. D., Kinzie, J., Schuh, J. H., Whitt, E. J., and Associates (2005). *Student success in college: Creating conditions that matter.* San Francisco: Jossey-Bass.

Kuh, G. D., and Love, P. G. (2000). A cultural perspective on student departure. In J. M. Braxton (Ed.), *Reworking the student departure puzzle* (pp. 196–212). Nashville, TN: Vanderbilt University Press.

Kuh, G. D., Nelson Laird, T. F., and Umbach, P. D. (2004). Aligning faculty activities and student behavior: Realizing the promise of greater expectations. *Liberal Education, 90*(4), 24–31.

Kuh, G. D., and Pascarella, E. T. (2004). What does institutional selectivity tell us about educational quality? *Change, 36*(5), 52–58.

Kuh, G. D., and Siegel, M. J. (2000). *College student experiences questionnaire: Tentative norms for the fourth edition.* Bloomington: Center for Postsecondary Research and Planning, Indiana University.

Kuh, G. D., and Umbach, P. D. (2004). College and character: Insights from the National Survey of Student Engagement. In J. Dalton and T. Russell (Eds.), *Assessing character outcomes in college.* New Directions in Institutional Research, Vol. 122 (pp. 37–54). San Francisco: Jossey-Bass.

Kuh, G. D., and Umbach, P. D. (2005). Experiencing diversity: What can we learn from liberal arts colleges? *Liberal Education, 91*(1), 14–21.

Kuh, G. D., and Whitt, E. J. (1988). *The invisible tapestry: Culture in American colleges and universities.* ASHE-ERIC Higher Education Report No. 1. Washington, DC: School of Education and Human Development, The George Washington University.

Kuh, G. D., and others. (1991). *Involving colleges: Successful approaches to fostering student learning and development outside the classroom.* San Francisco: Jossey-Bass.

Kuh, G. D., and others. (2006). *Connecting the dots: Multi-faceted analyses of the relationships between student engagement results from the NSSE, and the institutional practices and conditions that foster student success.* Bloomington, IN: Center for Postsecondary Research.

Kulik, J., Kulik, C., and Cohen, P. (1980). Effectiveness of computer-based college teaching: A meta-analysis of findings. *Review of Educational Research, 50*(4), 525–544.

Laden, B. V. (1999). Two-year Hispanic-serving colleges. In B. Townsend (Ed.), *Two-year colleges for women and minorities: Enabling access to the baccalaureate* (pp. 151–194). New York: Falmer Press.

Laden, B. V. (2001). Hispanic-serving institutions: Myths and realities. *Peabody Journal of Education, 76*(1), 73–92.

Laden, B. V. (2004). Hispanic-serving institutions: What are they? Where are they? *Community College Journal of Research and Practice, 28*(3), 181–198.

Lamont, M., and Lareau, J. (1988). Cultural capital: Allusions, gaps, and glissandos in recent theoretical developments. *Sociological Theory, 6*(2), 153–168.

Lamport, M. A. (1993). Student-faculty interaction and the effect on college student outcomes: A review of the literature. *Adolescence, 28*(112), 971–990.

Lenning, O. T, Beal, P., and Sauer, K. (1980). *Retention and attrition: Evidence for action and research.* Boulder, CO: National Center for Higher Education Management Systems.

Levine, A., and Cureton, J. S. (1998). Collegiate life: An obituary. *Change, 30*(3), 12–17.

Levine, A., and Nidiffer, J. (1996). *Beating the odds: How the poor get to college.* San Francisco: Jossey-Bass.

Lewis, C. W., and Middleton, V. (2003). African Americans in community colleges: A review of research reported in the *Community College Journal of Research and Practice:* 1990–2000. *Community College Journal of Research and Practice, 27*(9–10), 787–798.

Liddell, D. L., and Davis, T. L. (1996). The measure of moral orientation: Reliability and validity evidence. *Journal of College Student Development, 37*(5), 485–493.

London, H. B. (1989). Breaking away: A study of first-generation college students and their families. *American Journal of Education, 97*(1), 144–170.

London, H. B. (1992). Transformations: Cultural challenges faced by first-generation college students. *New Directions for Community Colleges, 20*(4), 5–11.

London, H. B., and Shaw, K. M. (1996). Enlarging the transfer paradigm: Practice and culture in the American community college. *Metropolitan Universities: An International Forum, 7*(2), 7–14.

Lucy-Allen, D., Merisotis, J., and Redmond, C. (2002). Developmental education and college opportunity in New England: Lessons for a national study of state and system policy impacts. Pilot study. Washington, DC: Institute for Higher Education Policy.

Mallinckrodt, B. (1988). Student retention, social support, and dropout intention: Comparison of black and white students. *Journal of College Student Development, 29*(1), 60–64.

Mallinckrodt, B., and Sedlacek, W. E. (1987). Student retention and the use of campus facilities by race. *NASPA Journal, 24*(3), 28–32.

Marchese, T. J. (1997). *The new conversations about learning.* Paper presented at the annual meeting of the American Association for Higher Education on Assessment and Quality, June, Miami Beach, FL.

Marchese, T. J. (1998). Not-so-distant competitors: How new providers are remaking the postsecondary marketplace. *AAHE Bulletin, 50*(9), 3–7.

Marsden, P. V. (2004). Social networks. In E. F. Borgatta and R.J.V. Montgomery (Eds.), *Encyclopedia of sociology,* Vol. 3 (2nd ed., pp. 2727–2735). New York: Macmillan Reference.

Marsh, H. (1984). Students' evaluations of university teaching: Dimensionality, reliability, validity, potential biases, and utility. *Journal of Educational Psychology, 76*(5), 707–754.

Martinez, M., and Klopott, S. (2003). *Improving college access for minority, low-income, and first-generation students.* Boston: Pathways to College Network.

Matthews, R. S. (1994). Enriching teaching and learning through learning communities. In T. O'Banion (Ed.), *Teaching and learning in the community college* (pp. 179–200). Washington, DC: Community College Press.

McCabe, R. H. (2000). *No one to waste: A report to public decision-makers and community college leaders.* Washington, DC: American Association of Community Colleges.

McCarthy, M. M., and Kuh, G. D. (2006). Are students ready for college? What student engagement data say. *Phi Delta Kappan, 87*(9), 664–669.

McCormick, A. C. (1990). *Mobility of educational expectations: The effect of community colleges.* Paper presented at the annual meeting of the Association for the Study of Higher Education, November, Portland, OR.

McCormick, A. C. (1997). *Transfer behavior among beginning postsecondary students: 1989–1994.* (NCES 97–266). Washington, DC: National Center for Education Statistics, U.S. Department of Education.

McCormick, A. C. (2003). Swirling and double-dipping: New patterns of student attendance and their implications for higher education. *New Directions for Higher Education
121*, 13–24.

McCormick, A. C., and Horn, L. J. (1996). *A descriptive summary of 1992–93 bachelor's
degree recipients: One year later.* (NCES 96–158). Washington, DC: National Center for
Education Statistics, U.S. Department of Education.

McDonough, P. M. (2004). *The school-to-college transition: Colleges and prospects.*
Washington, DC: Center for Policy Analysis, American Council on Education.

McKeachie, W. J., Pintrich, P. R., Lin, Y. G., and Smith, D.A.F. (1986). *Teaching and learning in the college classroom: A review of the research literature.* Ann Arbor: University of
Michigan.

Menges, R. J., and Mathis, B. C. (1988). Key resources on teaching, learning, curriculum,
and faculty development: A guide to the higher education literature. San Francisco:
Jossey-Bass.

Merton, R. K. (1948, Summer). The self-fulfilling prophecy. *Antioch Review,* 193–210.

Metzner, B. (1989). Perceived quality of academic advising: The effect on freshman attrition.
American Educational Research Journal, 26(3), 422–442.

Meyers, D., and others. (2004). *The impacts of regular Upward Bound: Results from the third
follow-up data collection.* (NCES 2004–13). Washington, DC: National Center for
Education Statistics, U.S. Department of Education.

Middle College National Consortium. (2006, May). *MCNC history.* Retrieved May 15,
2006, from http://www.lagcc.cuny.edu/mcnc/history.htm.

Miller, T., Kuh, G. D., Paine, D., and Associates. (2005). *Taking student expectations seriously:
A guide for campus applications.* San Francisco: Jossey-Bass.

Mortenson, T. G. (2003, August 9). *Fact sheet: What's wrong with the guys?* Retrieved April 7,
2006, from http://www.postsecondary.org/archives/previous/GuysFacts.pdf.

Mortenson, T. G. (2005, October). *Segregation of higher education enrollment by family
income and race/ethnicity: 1980 to 2004.* Oskaloosa, IA: Postsecondary Education
Opportunity.

Muraskin, L. (1997). *"Best practices" in student support services: A study of five exemplary sites.*
Washington, DC: Planning and Evaluation Service, U.S. Department of Education.

Muraskin, L. (2003). *National evaluation of GEAR UP: A summary of the first two years.*
Washington, DC: Department of Education.

Muraskin, L., and Lee, J., with Wilner, A., and Swail, W. S. (2004, December). *Raising the
graduation rates of low-income college students.* Washington, DC: Pell Institute for the
Study of Opportunity in Higher Education.

Muraskin, L., and Wilner, A. (2004). *What we know about institutional influences on retention.* Washington, DC: JBL Associates.

Murdock, T. A. (1990). Financial aid and persistence: An integrative review of the literature.
NASPA Journal: 27(3), 213–221.

Murray, D. M. (1985). *A writer teaches writing* (2nd Ed.). Boston: Houghton Mifflin Company.

National Articulation and Transfer Network. (2002). *National Articulation and Transfer Network: Building an alternative pathway for underserved student populations to access historically black colleges and universities, Hispanic serving institutions, and tribal colleges and universities.* San Francisco: City College of San Francisco.

National Association of Student Personnel Administrators, American Association for Higher Education, and American College Personnel Association. (1998). *Powerful partnerships: A shared responsibility for learning.* Washington, DC: National Association of Student Personnel Administrators, American Association for Higher Education, and American College Personnel Association.

National Association of Student Personnel Administrators and American College Personnel Association. (2004, January). *Learning reconsidered: A campus-wide focus on the student experience.* Washington, DC: National Association of Student Personnel Administrators and American College Personnel Association.

National Center for Public Policy and Higher Education. (2002, May). *Losing ground: A national status report on the affordability of American higher education.* San Jose, CA: National Center for Public Policy and Higher Education.

National Center for Public Policy and Higher Education. (2004a, September). *Measuring Up 2004: The national report card on higher education.* San Jose, CA: National Center for Public Policy and Higher Education.

National Center for Public Policy and Higher Education. (2004b, April). *Policy alert. The educational pipeline: Big investments, big returns.* San Jose, CA: National Center for Public Policy and Higher Education.

National Center for Public Policy and Higher Education. (2005, November). *Policy alert: Income of U.S. workforce projected to decline if education doesn't improve.* San Jose, CA: National Center for Public Policy and Higher Education.

National Research Council. (1999). *Equity and adequacy in education finance: Issues and perspectives.* Washington, DC: Committee on Education Finance, National Research Council.

National Research Council. (2000). *How people learn: Brain, mind, experience, and school.* Washington, DC: National Academies Press.

National Research Council. (2004). *Engaging schools: Fostering high school students' motivation to learn.* Washington, DC: National Academies Press.

National Survey of Student Engagement. (2000). *The NSSE 2000 report: National benchmarks of effective educational practice.* Bloomington: Center for Postsecondary Research, Indiana University.

National Survey of Student Engagement. (2001). *Improving the college experience: National benchmarks for effective educational practice.* Bloomington: Center for Postsecondary Research, Indiana University.

National Survey of Student Engagement. (2002). *From promise to progress: How colleges and universities are using student engagement results to improve collegiate quality.* Bloomington: Center for Postsecondary Research, Indiana University.

National Survey of Student Engagement. (2003). *Converting data into action: Expanding the boundaries of institutional improvement.* Bloomington: Center for Postsecondary Research, Indiana University.

National Survey of Student Engagement. (2004). *Student engagement: Pathways to collegiate success.* Bloomington: Center for Postsecondary Research, Indiana University.

National Survey of Student Engagement. (2005). *Student engagement: Exploring different dimensions of student engagement.* Bloomington: Center for Postsecondary Research, Indiana University.

Naumann, W. C., Bandalos, D., and Gutkin, T. B. (2003). Identifying variables that predict college success for first-generation college students. *Journal of College Admission, 181,* 4–9.

Nelson, R. B., Scott, T., and Bryan, W. (1984). Pre-college characteristics and early college experiences as predictors of freshman year persistence. *Journal of College Student Personnel, 25*(1), 50–54.

Nelson Laird, T. F., and Kuh, G. D. (2005). Student experiences with information technology and their relationship to other aspects of student engagement. *Research in Higher Education, 46*(2), 211–233.

Nettles, M. T., Wagener, U., Millett, C. M., and Killenbeck, A. M. (1999). Student retention and progression: A special challenge for private historically black colleges and universities. *New Directions for Higher Education, 27*(4), 51–67.

Newcomb, T. M. (1966). *The general nature of peer group influence.* In T. M. Newcomb and E. Wilson (Eds.), *College peer groups: Problems and prospects for research* (pp. 2–16). Chicago: Aldine Publishing Company.

Nora, A. (1999). *Community colleges in the 21st century: Revisiting and reexamining their mission.* Retrieved December 1, 2005, from http://199.75.76.16/initiatives/newexpeditions/white_papers/.

Nora, A., and Cabrera, A. F. (1996). The role of perceptions in prejudice and discrimination and the adjustment of minority students to college. *Journal of Higher Education, 67*(2), 119–148.

Nuñez, A. M. (1998). *First-generation students: A longitudinal analysis of educational and early labor market outcomes.* Paper presented at the annual meeting of the Association for the Study of Higher Education, November, Miami, FL.

Nuñez, A. M., and Cuccaro-Alamin, S. (1998). *First-generation students: Undergraduates whose parents never enrolled in postsecondary education* (NCES 98-082). Washington, DC: National Center for Education Statistics, U.S. Department of Education.

O'Brien, E. M., and Zudak, C. (1998). Minority-serving institutions: An overview. *New Directions for Higher Education, 26*(2), 5–15.

Olsen, D., and others. (1998). *Great expectations: What first-year students say they will do and what they actually do.* Paper presented at the annual meeting of the Association for the Study of Higher Education, November, Miami, FL.

Orfield, G. (2001). Introduction. In G. Orfield (Ed.), *Diversity challenged: Evidence on the impact of affirmative action* (pp. 1–30). Cambridge, MA: Harvard Education Publishing Group.

Ortiz, A. M. (2004). Promoting the success of Latino students: A call to action. In A. M. Ortiz (Ed.), *Addressing the unique needs of Latino American students.* New Directions for Student Services, Vol. 105 (pp. 89–97). San Francisco: Jossey-Bass.

Outcalt, C. L., and Skewes-Cox, T. E. (2002). Involvement, interaction, and satisfaction: The human environment at HBCUs. *Review of Higher Education, 25*(3), 331–347.

Pace, C. R. (1990). *The undergraduates: A report of their activities and college experiences in the 1980s.* Los Angeles: Center for the Study of Evaluation, UCLA Graduate School of Education.

Parrish, T. B., Matsumoto, C. S., and Fowler, W. J., Jr. (1995). *Disparities in public school district spending 1989–90: A multivariate, student-weighted analysis, adjusted for differences in geographic cost of living and student need.* Washington, DC: National Center for Education Statistics, U.S. Department of Education.

Pascarella, E. T. (1980). Student-faculty informal contact and college outcomes. *Review of Educational Research, 50*(4), 545–595.

Pascarella, E. T. (1985). College environmental influences on learning and cognitive development: A critical review and synthesis. In J. C. Smart (Ed.), *Higher education: Handbook of theory and research,* Vol. 1 (pp.1–62). New York: Agathon.

Pascarella, E. T. (2001). Cognitive growth in college: Surprising and reassuring findings. *Change, 33*(6), 20–27.

Pascarella, E. T., Bohr, L., Nora, A., and Terenzini, P. T. (1995). Cognitive effects of two-year and four-year colleges: New evidence. *Educational Evaluation and Policy Analysis, 17*(1), 83–96.

Pascarella, E. T., and Chapman, D. (1983). A multi-institutional, path analytic validation of Tinto's model of college withdrawal. *American Educational Research Journal, 20*(1), 87–102.

Pascarella, E. T., and others. (1996). Influences on students' openness to diversity and challenge in the first year of college. *Journal of Higher Education, 67*(2), 174–195.

Pascarella, E. T., and others. (1998). Does community college versus four-year college attendance influence students' educational plans? *Journal of College Student Development, 39*(2), 179–193.

Pascarella, E. T., and others. (2005). Institutional selectivity and good practices in undergraduate education. *Journal of Higher Education, 77*(2), 251–285.

Pascarella, E. T., Palmer, B., Moye, M., and Pierson, C. (2001). Do diversity experiences influence the development of critical thinking? *Journal of College Student Development, 42*(3), 257–271.

Pascarella, E. T., Pierson, C. T., Wolniak, G. C., and Terenzini, P. T. (2004). First generation college students: Additional evidence on college experiences and outcomes. *Journal of Higher Education, 75*(3), 249–284.

Pascarella, E. T., Smart, J. C., and Ethington, C. A. (1986). Long-term persistence of two-year college students. *Research in Higher Education, 24*(1), 47–71.

Pascarella, E. T., and Terenzini, P. T. (1976). Informal interaction with faculty and freshman ratings of academic and nonacademic experience of college. *Journal of Educational Research, 70*(1), 35–41.

Pascarella, E. T., and Terenzini, P. T. (1979a). Interaction effects in Spady's and Tinto's conceptual models of college dropout. *Sociology of Education, 52*(4), 197–210.

Pascarella, E. T., and Terenzini, P. T. (1979b). Student-faculty informal contact and college persistence: A further investigation. *Journal of Educational Research, 72*(4), 214–218.

Pascarella, E. T., and Terenzini, P. T. (1983). Predicting voluntary freshman year persistence/withdrawal behavior in a residential university: A path analytic validation of Tinto's model. *Journal of Educational Psychology, 75*(2), 215–226.

Pascarella, E. T., and Terenzini, P. T. (1991). *How college affects students: Findings and insights from twenty years of research.* San Francisco: Jossey-Bass.

Pascarella, E. T., and Terenzini, P. T. (1995). The impact of college on students: Myths, rational myths, and some other things that may not be true. *NACADA Journal, 15*(2), 26–33.

Pascarella, E .T., and Terenzini, P. T. (2005). *How college affects students: A third decade of research.* San Francisco: Jossey-Bass.

Pathways to College Network. (2004). *A shared agenda: A leadership challenge to improve college access and success.* Boston: Education Resources Institute.

Pell Institute. (2004). *Indicators of opportunity in higher education: Fall 2004 status report.* Washington, DC: Pell Institute.

Pennington, H. (2004, December). *Fast track to college: Increasing postsecondary success for all students.* Boston: Jobs for the Future.

Perna, L. W., and Titus, M. A. (2005). The relationship between parental involvement as social capital and college enrollment: An examination of racial/ethnic group differences. *Journal of Higher Education, 76*(5), 485–518.

Peter, K. and Cataldi, E. F. (2005). *The road less traveled? Students who enroll in multiple institutions.* (NCES 2005–157). Washington, DC: National Center for Education Statistics, U.S. Department of Education.

Pierce, C. M. (1989). Unity in diversity: Thirty-three years of stress. In G. L. Berry and J. K. Asamen (Eds.), *Black students: Psychological issues and academic achievement* (pp. 296–312). Newbury Park, CA: Sage.

Pike, G. R. (1991). *Dimensions of academic growth and development during college: Using alumni reports to evaluate education programs.* Paper presented at the annual meeting of the Association for the Student of Higher Education, November, Boston, MA.

Pike, G. R. (1993). The relationship between perceived learning and satisfaction with college: An alternative view. *Research in Higher Education, 34*(1), 23–40.

Pike, G. R. (1999). The effects of residential learning communities and traditional residential living arrangements on educational gains during the first year of college. *Journal of College Student Development, 40*(3), 269–284.

Pike, G. R. (2003). Membership in a fraternity or sorority, student engagement, and educational outcomes at AAU public research universities. *Journal of College Student Development, 44*(3), 369–382.

Pike, G. R. (2004). Measuring quality: A comparison of *U.S. News* rankings and NSSE benchmarks. *Research in Higher Education, 45*(2), 193–208.

Pike, G. R., and Askew, J. W. (1990). The impact of fraternity or sorority membership on academic involvement and learning outcomes. *NASPA Journal, 28*(1), 13–19.

Pike, G. R., and Kuh, G. D. (2005a). First- and second-generation college students: A comparison of their engagement and intellectual development. *Journal of Higher Education, 76*(3), 276–300.

Pike, G. R., and Kuh, G. D. (2005b). A typology of student engagement for American colleges and universities. *Research in Higher Education, 46*(2), 185–209.

Pike, G. R., and Kuh, G. D. (2006). Another look at the relationships among structural diversity, informal peer interactions, and perceptions of the campus environment. *Review of Higher Education, 29*(4), 425–450.

Pike, G. R., Kuh, G. D., and Gonyea, R. M. (2003). The relationship between institutional mission and students' involvement and educational outcomes. *Research in Higher Education, 44*(2), 243–263.

Pike, G. R., and Saupe, J. L. (2002). Does high school matter? An analysis of three methods of predicting first-year grades. *Research in Higher Education, 43*(2), 187–207.

Pike, G. R., Schroeder, C. C., and Berry, T. R. (1997). Enhancing the educational impact of residence halls: The relationship between residential learning communities and first-year college experiences and persistence. *Journal of College Student Development, 38*(6), 609–621.

Pike, G. R., Smart, J. C., Kuh, G. D., and Hayek, J. C. (2006). Educational expenditures and student engagement: When does money matter? *Research in Higher Education, 47*(7), 847–872.

Porter, O. F. (1990). *Undergraduate completion and persistence at four-year colleges and universities: Completers, persisters, stopouts, and dropouts.* Paper presented at the annual meeting of the American Educational Research Association, April, Boston, MA.

Pounds, A. (1987). Black students' needs on predominantly white campuses. *New Directions for Student Services, 38,* 23–38.

Presley, J. B., and Clery, S. B. (2001). Middle-income undergraduates: Where they enroll and how they pay for their education. *Education Statistics Quarterly, 3*(3), 78–81.

Price, D. V. (2005). *Learning communities and student success in postsecondary education: A background paper.* New York: MDRC.

Provasnik, S., and Shafer, L. L. (2004). *Historically black colleges and universities: 1976 to 2001.* (NCES 2004–062). Washington, DC: National Center for Education Statistics. U.S. Department of Education.

Reason, R. D., Terenzini, P. T., and Domingo, R. J. (2005). *First things first: Developing academic competence in the first year of college.* Paper presented at the annual meeting of the Association for Institutional Research, May, San Diego, CA.

Redd, K. E. (2001). *Discounting toward disaster: Tuition discounting, college finances, and enrollments of low-income undergraduates.* New Agenda Series, Vol. 3, No. 2. Indianapolis: USA Group Foundation.

Rendon, L. I. (1994a). *Beyond involvement: Creating validating academic and social communities in the community college.* Paper presented at the American River Community College, August, Sacramento, CA.

Rendon, L. I. (1994b). *A systemic view of minority students in educational institutions.* Paper presented at the Southern Education Foundation Panel on Educational Opportunity and Postsecondary Desegregation, February, Austin, TX.

Rendon, L. I. (1995). *Facilitating retention and transfer for first generation students in community colleges.* Paper presented at the New Mexico Institute, Rural Community College Initiative, March, Espanola, NM.

Rendon, L. I. (1998). *Access in a democracy: Narrowing the opportunity gap.* Paper presented at the Policy Panel on Access, National Postsecondary Education Cooperative, September, Washington, DC.

Rendon, L. I. (1999). Toward a new vision of the multicultural community college for the next century. In K. M. Shaw, J. R. Valadez, and R. A. Rhoads (Eds.), *Community colleges as cultural texts: Qualitative explorations of organizational and student culture* (pp. 195–204). Albany: State University of New York Press.

Rendon, L. I., and Garza, H. (1996). Closing the gap between two- and four-year institutions. In L. I. Rendon and R. Hope (Eds.), *Educating a new majority* (pp. 289–308). San Francisco: Jossey-Bass.

Rendon, L. I., Jalomo, R. E., and Nora, A. (2000). Theoretical consideration in the study of minority student retention in higher education. In J. M. Braxton (Ed.), *Rethinking the departure puzzle: New theory and research on college student retention* (pp. 127–156). Nashville, TN: Vanderbilt University Press.

Reynolds, A. J., and Walberg, H. J. (1992). A process model of mathematics achievement and attitude. *Journal for Research in Mathematics Education, 23*(4), 306–328.

Richardson, R. C., and Skinner, E. F. (1992). Helping first-generation minority students achieve degrees. *New Directions for Community Colleges, 20*(4), 29–43.

Rifkin, T. (1998). *Issues surrounding the community college collegiate function: A synthesis of the literature.* Los Angeles: ERIC Clearinghouse for Community Colleges.

Roach, R. (2000). Ambitious outreach. *Black Issues in Higher Education, 17*(12), 19.

Rosenbaum, J. (1998, October). *Unrealistic plans and misdirected efforts: Are community colleges getting the right message to high school students?* (Community College Research Center Occasional Paper). New York: Community College Research Center, Teachers College, Columbia University.

Rousseau, D. M. (1995). *Psychological contract in organizations: Understanding written and unwritten agreements.* Newbury Park, CA: Sage.

Russel, J. H., and Skinkle, R. R. (1990). Evaluation of peer-adviser effectiveness. *Journal of College Student Development, 31*(5), 388–394.

Rutherford, F. J., and Ahlgren, A. (1990). *Science for all Americans.* New York: Oxford University Press.

St. John, E. P. (2002). *The access challenge: Rethinking the causes of the new inequality.* (Policy Issues Report). Bloomington: Education Policy Center, Indiana University.

St. John, E. P. (2003). *Refinancing the college dream: Access, equal opportunity, and justice for taxpayers.* Baltimore: Johns Hopkins University Press.

St. John, E. P., Hu, S., Simmons, A., and Musoba, G. D. (1999). *Aptitude versus merit: What matters in persistence?* (Policy Research Report). Bloomington: Education Policy Center, Indiana University.

St. John, E. P., Paulsen, M. B., and Carter, D. F. (2005). Diversity, college costs, and postsecondary opportunity: An examination of the financial nexus between college choice and persistence for African Americans and whites. *Journal of Higher Education,* 76(5), 545–569.

Saupe, J. L., Smith, T. Y., and Xin, W. (1999). *Institutional and student characteristics in student success: First-term GPA, one-year retention and six-year graduation.* Paper presented at the annual meeting for the Association for Institutional Research, May, Seattle, WA.

Sax, L. J., and others. (2003). *The American freshman: National norms for fall 2003.* Los Angeles: Higher Education Research Institute, University of California, Los Angeles.

Schilling, K. M., and Schilling, K. L. (1999). Increasing expectations for student effort. *About Campus,* 4(2), 4–10.

Schmit, J. (1991). *An empirical look at the search stage of the student college choice process.* Paper presented at the annual meeting of the Association for the Study of Higher Education, November, Boston, MA.

Schroeder, C. C., and Hurst, J. C. (1996). Designing learning environments that integrate curricular and cocurricular experiences. *Journal of College Student Development,* 37(2), 174–181.

Schroeder, C. C., Minor, F. D., and Tarkow, T. A. (1999). Freshman interest groups: partnerships for promoting student success. *New Directions for Student Services* (87), 37–49.

Shapiro, N. S., and Levine, J. H. (1999). *Creating learning communities: A practical guide to winning support, organizing for change, and implementing programs.* San Francisco: Jossey-Bass.

Shaw, K. M., and London, H. B. (2001). Culture and ideology in keeping transfer commitment: Three community colleges. *Review of Higher Education,* 25(1), 91–114.

Shulman, J., and Bowen, W. (2001). *The game of life: College sports and educational values.* Princeton, NJ: Princeton University Press.

Simpson, C., Baker, K., and Mellinger, G. (1980). Convention failures and unconventional dropouts: Comparing different types of university withdrawals. *Sociology of Education,* 53(4), 203–214.

Smart, J. C., Feldman, K. A., and Ethington, C. A. (2000). *Academic disciplines: Holland's theory and the study of college students and faculty.* Nashville, TN: Vanderbilt University Press.

Snyder, M., and Swann, W. B. (1978). Behavioral confirmation in social interaction: From social perception to social reality. *Journal of Experimental Social Psychology,* 14(2), 148–162.

Social Science Research Council Project. (2005). *Questions that matter: Setting the research agenda on access and success in postsecondary education.* New York: Social Science Research Council Project Transitions to College: From Theory to Practice.

Solorzano, D. G. (1995). The doctorate production and baccalaureate origins of African Americans in the sciences and engineering. *Journal of Negro Education,* 64(1), 15–32.

Sorcinelli, M. D. (1991). Research findings on the seven principles. *New Directions for Teaching and Learning,* 47, 13–25.

Spady, W. G. (1970). Dropouts from higher education: An interdisciplinary review and synthesis. *Interchange, 1*(1), 64–85.

Stage, F. K. (1989). An alternative to path analysis: A demonstration of LISREL using students' commitment to an institution. *Journal of College Student Development, 30*(2), 129–135.

Stage, F. K., and Hossler, D. (2000). Where is the student? Linking student behaviors, college choice, and college persistence. In J. M. Braxton (Ed.), *Reworking the student departure puzzle* (pp. 170–195). Nashville, TN: Vanderbilt University Press.

State Higher Education Executive Officers. (2005). Accountability for better results—a national imperative for higher education. *Network News, 24*(1), 1–4.

Steadman, M. H. (1998). CATs: Using classroom assessment to change both teaching and learning. *New Directions for Teaching and Learning, 75*, 23–35.

Stern, G. (1970). *People in context: Measuring person-environment congruence in education and industry.* New York: Wiley.

Sternberg, R. J. (2005). Accomplishing the goals of affirmative action—with or without affirmative action. *Change, 37*(1), 6–14.

Stoecker, J. L., Pascarella, E. T., and Wolfe, L. (1988). Persistence in higher education: A nine-year test of a theoretical model. *Journal of College Student Development, 29*(3), 196–209.

Strange, C., and Banning, J. (2001). *Educating by design: Creating campus learning environments that work.* San Francisco: Jossey-Bass.

Strauss, L. C., and Volkwein, J. F. (2002). Comparing student performance and growth in two- and four-year institutions. *Research in Higher Education, 43*(2), 133–161.

Strumpf, G., and Hunt, P. (1993). The effects of an orientation course on the retention and academic standing of entering freshmen, controlling for the volunteer effect. *Journal of the Freshman Year Experience, 5*(1), 7–14.

Suarez, A. L. (2003). Forward transfer: Strengthening the educational pipeline for Latino community college students. *Community College Journal of Research and Practice, 27*(2), 95–118.

Swail, W. S., with Redd, K. E., and Perna, L. W. (2003). *Retaining minority students in higher education: A framework for success.* ASHE-ERIC Higher Education Report No. 2. Washington, DC: School of Education and Human Development, The George Washington University.

Swail, W. S., Cabrera, A. F., Lee, C., and Williams, A. (2005). Latino students and the educational pipelines: A three-part series. Part III: Pathways to the bachelor's degree for Latino students. Stafford, VA: Education Policy Institute.

Swanson, C. (2002). *Cooling-out and warming-up: The role of the postsecondary institutional environment in managing ambitions.* Unpublished manuscript. Chicago: National Opinion Research Center, University of Chicago.

Tagg, J. (2003). *The learning paradigm college.* Bolton, MA: Anker Publishing Company.

Taylor, K., with Moore, W. S., MacGregor, J., and Lindblad, J. (2003). *Learning community research and assessment: What we know now.* National Learning Communities Project

Monograph Series. Olympia, WA: Washington Center for Improving the Quality of Undergraduate Education, Evergreen State College.

Terenzini, P. T., Pascarella, E. T., and Blimling, G. S. (1996). Students' out-of-class experiences and their influence on learning and cognitive development: A literature review. *Journal of College Student Development, 37*(2), 149–162.

Terenzini, P. T., Springer, L., Pascarella, E. T., and Nora, A. (1995). Academic and out-of-class influences on students' intellectual development. *Review of Higher Education, 19*(1), 23–44.

Terenzini, P. T., and others. (1994). The transition to college: Diverse students, diverse stories. *Research in Higher Education, 35*(1), 57–73.

Terenzini, P. T., and others. (1996). First-generation college students: Characteristics, experiences, and cognitive development. *Research in Higher Education, 37*(1), 1–22.

Terenzini, P. T., and others. (1997). *African American college students' experiences in HBCUs and PWIs and learning outcomes.* University Park, PA: National Center on Postsecondary Teaching, Learning, and Assessment.

Tierney, W. G. (1992). *Official encouragement, institutional discouragement: Minorities in academe—the Native American experience.* Norwood, NJ: Ablex Publishing Corporation.

Tierney, W. G. (1993). *Building communities of difference: Higher education in the twenty-first century.* Westport, CT: Bergin & Garvey.

Tierney, W. G. (1999). *Building the responsive campus: Creating high performance colleges and universities.* Thousand Oaks, CA: Sage.

Tierney, W. G., Corwin, Z. B., and Colyar, J. E. (Eds.). (2005). *Preparing for college: Nine elements for effective outreach.* Albany: State University of New York Press.

Tierney, W. G., and Hagedorn, L. S. (2002). *Increasing access to college: Extending possibilities for all students.* Albany: State University of New York Press.

Tinto, V. (1975). Dropout from higher education: A theoretical synthesis of recent research. *Review of Educational Research, 45*(1), 89–125.

Tinto, V. (1986). Theories of student departure revisited. In J.C. Smart (Ed.), *Higher education: Handbook of theory and research* (Vol. 2, pp. 359–384). New York: Agathon.

Tinto, V. (1987). *Leaving college: Rethinking the causes and cures of student attrition.* Chicago: University of Chicago Press.

Tinto, V. (1993). *Leaving college: Rethinking the causes and cures of student attrition* (2nd ed.). Chicago: University of Chicago Press.

Tinto, V. (1996). Reconstructing the first year of college. *Planning for Higher Education, 25*(1), 1–6.

Tinto, V. (1997a). Classrooms as communities: Exploring the educational character of student persistence. *Journal of Higher Education, 68*(6), 599–623.

Tinto, V. (1997b). Enhancing learning via community. *Thought and Action, 13*(1), 53–58.

Tinto, V. (2004). *Student retention and graduation: Facing the truth, living with the consequences.* Occasional Paper No. 1. Washington, DC: Pell Institution for the Study of Opportunity in Higher Education.

Tinto, V., and Love, A. G. (1995). *A longitudinal study of learning communities at LaGuardia community college.* University Park, PA: National Center on Postsecondary Teaching, Learning, and Assessment.

Tinto, V., Love, A. G, and Russo, P. (1995). *Building learning communities for new students: A summary of research findings of the collaborative learning project.* University Park, PA: National Center on Postsecondary Teaching, Learning, and Assessment.

Titus, M. A. (2004). An examination of the influence of institutional context on student persistence at four-year colleges and universities: A multilevel approach. *Research in Higher Education, 45*(7), 673–699.

Torres, V. (2003). Influences on ethnic identity development of Latino college students in the first two years of college. *Journal of College Student Development, 44*(4), 532–547.

Townsend, B. K. (1995). Community college transfer students: A case study of survival. *Review of Higher Education, 18*(2), 175–193.

Treisman, U. (1992). Studying students studying calculus: A look at the lives of minority mathematics students in college. *College Mathematics Journal, 23*(5), 362–372.

Trow, M. (2001). From mass higher education to universal access: The American advantage. In P. G. Altbach, P. J. Gumport, and D. B. Johnstone (Eds.), *In defense of American higher education* (pp. 110–143). Baltimore: Johns Hopkins University Press.

Turner, C.S.V. (1988). *A California case study: Organizational determinants of the transfer of Hispanic students from two- to four-year colleges.* Unpublished doctoral dissertation, Stanford University.

Turner, C.S.V. (1994). Guests in someone else's house: Students of color. *Review of Higher Education, 17*(4), 355–370.

Twigg, C. A. (2002). *Redefining community: Small colleges in the information age.* Paper presented at the Pew Symposium in Learning and Technology, October, Charleston, SC.

Twigg, C. A. (2003). Improving quality and reducing cost: Designs for effective learning. *Change, 35*(4), 22–29.

Twigg, C. A. (2005). *Improving learning and reducing costs: New models for online learning.* Keynote address at the annual meeting of the Association for Learning Technology, July, Manchester, England.

Tym, C., McMillion, R., Barone, S., and Webster, J. (2004). *First-generation college students: A literature review* (Research and Analytic Services). Texas Round Rock: Texas Guaranteed Student Loan Corporation.

Umbach, P. D, and Kuh, G. D. (2004). Disengaged jocks: Myth or reality? *LiberalArtsOnline, 4*(4). Retrieved January 3, 2006, from http://staged.wabash.edu/cila/displayStory_print.cfm?news_ID=1593.

Umbach, P. D., and Kuh, G. D. (2006). Student experiences with diversity at liberal arts colleges: Another claim for distinctiveness. *Journal of Higher Education, 77*(1), 169–192.

Umbach, P. D., Palmer, M. M., Kuh, G. D., and Hannah, S. J. (2004). *Intercollegiate athletes and effective educational practices: Winning combination or losing effort?* Paper presented at the annual meeting of the Association for Institutional Research, June, Boston, MA.

U.S. Department of Education. (1997). *Findings from the* Condition of Education, 1996: *Minorities in higher education.* (NCES 97–372). Washington, DC: National Center for Education Statistics.

U.S. Department of Education. (2003a). *Digest of education statistics, 2002.* (NCES 2003–060). Washington, DC: National Center for Education Statistics.

U.S. Department of Education. (2003b). *High schools with high expectations for all.* Issue Paper: The High School Leadership Summit. Washington, DC: U.S. Department of Education.

U.S. Department of Education. (2004). *The condition of education, 2004.* (NCES 2004–077). Washington, DC: National Center for Education Statistics, U.S. Department of Education.

U.S. Department of Education. (2006). *A test of leadership: Charting the future of U.S. higher education.* Washington, DC: U.S. Department of Education. Retrieved October 1, 2006, from www.ed.gov/about/bdscomm/list/hiedfuture/reports/final-report.pdf.

University of Texas at El Paso. (2003). *A longitudinal study of student persistence in science, technology, engineering, and mathematics (STEM) at a regional urban university.* El Paso: University of Texas at El Paso.

Upcraft, M. L., Gardner, J. N., and Barefoot, B. O. (2005). *Challenging and supporting the first-year student: A handbook for improving the first year of college.* San Francisco: Jossey-Bass.

Upcraft, M. L., Mullendore, R. H., Borefoot, B. O., and Fidler, D. S. (1993). *Designing successful transitions: A guide for orienting students to college.* Monograph No. 13. Columbia, SC: National Orientation Directors Association, National Resource Center for the Freshman Year Experience, University of South Carolina.

Van Gennep, A. (1960). *The rites of passage.* Chicago: University of Chicago Press.

Venezia, A., and others. (2005). *The governance divide: A report on a four-state study on improving college readiness and success.* San Jose, CA: The Institute for Educational Leadership, the National Center for Public Policy and Higher Education, and the Stanford Institute for Higher Education Research.

Venezia, A., Kirst, M. W., and Antonio, A. L. (2003). *Betraying the college dream: How disconnected K–12 and postsecondary education systems undermine student aspirations.* Stanford, CA: National Center for Postsecondary Improvement.

Volkwein, J. F., and Cabrera, A. F. (1998). *Student measures associated with favorable classroom experiences.* Paper presented at the annual meeting of the Association for Institutional Research, May, Minneapolis, MN.

Volkwein, J. F., and Carbone, D. A. (1994). The impact of departmental research and teaching climates on undergraduate growth and satisfaction. *Journal of Higher Education, 65*(2), 147–167.

Volkwein, J. F., and others. (2000). *A multicampus study of academic performance and cognitive growth among native freshman, two-year transfers, and four-year transfers.* Paper presented at the annual meeting of the Association for Institutional Research, May, Cincinnati, OH.

Voorhees, R. (1987). Toward building models of community college persistence: A logit analysis. *Research in Higher Education, 26*(2), 115–129.

Wang, H., and Grimes, J. W. (2001). A systematic approach to assessing retention programs: Identifying critical points for meaningful interventions and validating outcomes assessment. *Journal of College Student Retention, 2*(1), 59–68.

Warburton, E. C., Bugarin, R., and Nuñez, A. M. (2001). Bridging the gap: Academic preparation and postsecondary success of first-generation students. *Education Statistics Quarterly, 3*(3), 73–77.

Watkins, T. J. (1997). Teacher communications, child achievement, and parent traits in parent involvement models. *Journal of Educational Research, 91*(l), 3–14.

Watson, L. W., and Kuh, G. D. (1996). The influence of dominant race environments on student involvement, perceptions, and educational gains: A look at historically black and predominantly white liberal arts institutions. *Journal of College Student Development, 37*(4), 415–424.

Weiler, W. (1993). Post baccalaureate educational choices of minority students. *Review of Higher Education, 16*(4), 439–460.

Wenglinsky, H. (1998). Finance equalization and within-school equity: The relationship between education spending and the social distribution of achievement. *Educational Evaluation and Policy Analysis, 20*(4), 269–283.

Western Interstate Commission for Higher Education. (2003, May). *What is changing direction? A project overview.* Boulder, CO: Western Interstate Commission for Higher Education.

Western Washington University. (1996). *Law and diversity program. Report to the Fund for the Improvement of Postsecondary Education (FIPSE).* Retrieved May 26, 2006, from http://www.ac.wwu.edu/~ldp/.

Whiteley, J. (1982). *Character development in college students* (Vol. 1). Schenectady, NY: Character Research Press.

Whitt, E. J. (1994). "I can be anything!": Student leadership in three women's colleges. *Journal of College Student Development, 35*(3), 198–207.

Whitt, E. J., and others. (2001). Influences on students' openness to diversity and challenge in the second and third years of college. *Journal of Higher Education, 72*(2), 172–204.

Wilkinson, R. (2005, October 7). What colleges must do to help needy students. *Chronicle of Higher Education,* B7.

York-Anderson, D., and Bowman, S. (1991). Assessing the college knowledge of first-generation and second-generation students. *Journal of College Student Development, 32*(2), 116–122.

Zhao, C-M., and Kuh, G. D., (2004). Adding value: Learning communities and student engagement. *Research in Higher Education, 45*(2), 115–138.

Zhao, C-M., Kuh, G. D., and Carini, R. M. (2005). A comparison of international student and American student engagement in effective educational practices. *Journal of Higher Education, 76*(2), 209–232.

Name Index

Dinham, S., 59
Domingo, R. J., 54, 79
Dougherty, K. J., 76
Douglas, K. B., 8, 14, 56, 91, 98, 120
Duch, B., 94
Dunphy, L., 79
Dweck, C. S., 16, 17, 36, 109, 119

E

Eaton, S., 16
Ebert-May, D., 94
Eckland, B. K., 59
Ehrenberg, R. G., 78
Eimers, M. T., 100, 101
Epps, E., 56
Ethington, C. A., 56, 60, 99
Ewell, P. T., 54, 75, 76, 127

F

Fallows, J., 4
Feagin, J. R., 62
Feldman, D. C., 36, 37
Feldman, K. A., 54, 93, 99
Fermin, B. J., 112
Fidler, D. S., 79
Fidler, P. P., 79
Finn, C. E. Jr., 106
Finney, J. E., 113
Fischer, N. M., 32
Fitzgerald, B. K., 128
Forest, A., 79, 116
Fowler, W. J., Jr., 24
Friedman, R. J., 35
Fries-Britt, S., 55
Frost, S., 106

G

Gamson, Z. F., 12, 43, 69, 90, 91, 95, 120
Ganderton, P., 41
Ganeshananthan, V. V., 4
Garcia, P., 62
Gardner, J. N., 79, 80, 86
Garza, H., 76, 77
Gerken, J. T., 43, 44
Gladieux, L. E., 25, 27, 34, 106

Gleason, P., 29
Godwin, G. J., 75
Golde, C., 85
Goldin, C., 19, 22
Goldschmid, B., 58
Goldschmid, M., 58
Gonyea, R. M., 37, 38, 76
Gonzales, J. L., Jr., 2
Gonzalez, J. M., 2
Gonzalez, K. P., 17, 18
Gonzalez, N. A., 35
Gonzalez-Vasquez, N., 55, 77, 78
Goodsell, A. S., 66
Gordon, E. W., 113
Graunke, S. S., 55
Grimes, J. W., 116
Gron, S. E., 94
Grubb, W. N., 88, 120
Guerin, K., 41
Gumport, P., 78, 90
Gur, R., 58
Gurin, C., 70, 73
Gurin, P. Y., 56, 59, 70, 73
Guskin, A. E., 90, 94
Gutierrez, R., 33
Gutkin, T. B., 32

H

Hagedorn, L. S., 109, 111
Hamrick, F. A., 24, 29, 32, 33
Hanks, M. P., 59
Hannah, S. J., 65
Hanniford, B., 41
Harker, R. K., 18
Harvey, W. B., 2
Hassel, H., 92
Hayek, J. C., 64, 65, 74
Hearn, J. C., 56
Heath, T., 78
Hechinger, F. M., 1
Hedlund, D., 88
Heller, D. E., 29, 45, 46, 113, 128
Helmcamp, A., 86
Hengstler, D., 9, 19
Hernandez, J. C., 63, 101
Himelhock, C. R., 55

Swail, W. S., 2, 9, 25, 27, 28, 30, 32–35, 39, 40, 88, 100, 106, 128
Swann, W. B., 36
Swanson, C., 40
Szecsy, E. M., 2

T

Tagg, J., 81, 90, 92, 94, 95
Tarkow, T. A., 86, 100
Taylor, K., 83–85
Terenzini, P. T., 1, 8–10, 12, 13, 15, 17, 20, 30–32, 37, 38, 40, 41, 43–46, 50, 52, 54, 56–60, 69, 71, 72, 76–80, 83, 89, 90, 93, 98, 113, 123, 124
Terry, B. T., 30
Tierney, W. G., 17, 33, 109, 111, 120, 121, 128
Tinto, V., 13–15, 17, 19, 20, 38, 54, 58, 60, 82, 83, 86, 117, 123, 124
Titus, M. A., 32, 33, 72
Torres, V., 18, 121
Townsend, B. K., 77
Treisman, U., 91
Trow, M., 1
Tsui, L., 77, 78
Turner, B., 28, 55, 77
Turner, C. S. V., 62
Twigg, C. A., 57, 96, 97, 120
Tym, C., 31

U

Umbach, P. D., 53, 59, 65, 73, 74, 100
Upcraft, M. L., 79, 80

V

Van Gennep, A., 13
Venezia, A., 7, 32, 106, 107, 109, 124
Vera, H., 62
Vesper, N., 35, 37, 60, 61, 110, 111
Volkwein, J. F., 8, 43, 44, 73, 93, 99, 102
Voorhees, R., 56

W

Wagener, U., 81, 101
Wahlberg, H. J., 24
Walker, M. T., 78
Wang, H., 116
Warburton, E. C., 29, 30, 32, 34
Watkins, T. J., 25
Watson, L. W., 101
Watt, J. D., 66
Webster, J., 31
Weiler, W., 78
Wenglinsky, H., 25, 35, 78
Whitely, J., 37
Whitmore, R. W., 3
Whitt, E. J., 15, 17, 28, 44, 60, 69, 73, 76, 79, 81, 89, 92, 94, 95, 98, 99, 101, 102, 116, 118–120, 122, 127, 128
Wilkinson, R., 109
Williams, A., 9, 25, 30, 32, 33, 35, 40, 88, 128
Williams, J. M., 37, 38
Wilner, A., 39, 79
Wilson, R., 23
Wolfe, L., 56
Wolniak, G. C., 9, 31, 76, 95
Woodruff, R., 79
Woosley, S. A., 55
Wright, I., 41

X

Xin, W., 71

Y

York-Anderson, D., 32

Z

Zhao, C-M., 63, 67, 84
Zudak, C., 35, 62

Subject Index

University of Idaho, 57
University of Maryland, College Park, 80
University of Michigan, 118, 122
University of South Carolina, 117
University of Southern Mississippi, 97
University of Texas, El Paso, 1, 85, 119
University of the Incarnate Word, 1
Upward Bound, 112
Upward Bound Math/Science, 112

V

Virginia Tech, 57

W

Western Interstate Commission for
    Education, 113
Western Washington University, 85
Wheaton College, 116
Winston-Salem State University, 119
World War II, 22
Wyoming, 2

X

Xavier University, 119

About the Authors

George D. Kuh is Chancellor's Professor of Higher Education at Indiana University, Bloomington, where he directs the Center for Postsecondary Research, home to the National Survey of Student Engagement and related initiatives. A past president of the Association for the Study of Higher Education, Kuh has written extensively about student engagement, assessment, institutional improvement, and college and university cultures and has consulted with more than 185 educational institutions and agencies in the United States and abroad.

Jillian Kinzie is associate director of the NSSE Institute for Effective Educational Practice and the Indiana University Center for Postsecondary Research. Her Ph.D. in higher education with a minor in women's studies is from Indiana University Bloomington. Previously she was coordinator of the master's program in higher education and student affairs at Indiana University and worked in academic and student affairs administration at Miami University of Ohio. She is coauthor of *Student Success in College: Creating Conditions that Matter* (Jossey-Bass, 2005) and *One Size Does Not Fit All: Traditional and Innovative Models of Student Affairs Practice* (Routledge, 2006).

Jennifer A. Buckley is a Ph.D. candidate in higher education and student affairs with a minor in inquiry methodology at Indiana University. She received her B.A. in political science from Gettysburg College and her M.A. in college student personnel from Miami University of Ohio. Currently, she works with the Center for Postsecondary Research and the National Survey of Student Engagement Institute. Her research interests include human learning and development, teaching and learning environments, and faculty-student interactions.

Brian K. Bridges is associate director for the Center for Advancement of Racial and Ethnic Equity at the American Council on Education and assistant professorial lecturer of higher education administration at The George Washington University. Previously, he was an associate director of the Indiana University Center for Postsecondary Research, where he coordinated the Building Engagement and Attainment of Minority Students Project. He also was a student affairs administrator at Western Carolina University and worked with TRIO programs at the University of North Carolina at Charlotte and at Indiana University.

John C. Hayek is associate vice president for planning and performance for the Kentucky Council on Postsecondary Education. For 2006–2007, he also is a program associate at the National Center on Public Policy in Higher Education. Previously, he was senior associate director of the Indiana University Center for Postsecondary Research and the National Survey of Student Engagement. In addition, he has held management positions in the not-for-profit sector. His undergraduate degree is from the University of Chicago and his Ph.D. in higher education is from Indiana University.

About the ASHE Higher Education Report Series

Since 1983, the ASHE (formerly ASHE-ERIC) Higher Education Report Series has been providing researchers, scholars, and practitioners with timely and substantive information on the critical issues facing higher education. Each monograph presents a definitive analysis of a higher education problem or issue, based on a thorough synthesis of significant literature and institutional experiences. Topics range from planning to diversity and multiculturalism, to performance indicators, to curricular innovations. The mission of the Series is to link the best of higher education research and practice to inform decision making and policy. The reports connect conventional wisdom with research and are designed to help busy individuals keep up with the higher education literature. Authors are scholars and practitioners in the academic community. Each report includes an executive summary, review of the pertinent literature, descriptions of effective educational practices, and a summary of key issues to keep in mind to improve educational policies and practice.

The Series is one of the most peer reviewed in higher education. A National Advisory Board made up of ASHE members reviews proposals. A National Review Board of ASHE scholars and practitioners reviews completed manuscripts. Six monographs are published each year and they are approximately 120 pages in length. The reports are widely disseminated through Jossey-Bass and John Wiley & Sons, and they are available online to subscribing institutions through Wiley InterScience (http://www.interscience.wiley.com).

Call for Proposals

The ASHE Higher Education Report Series is actively looking for proposals. We encourage you to contact one of the editors, Dr. Kelly Ward (kaward@wsu.edu) or Dr. Lisa Wolf-Wendel (lwolf@ku.edu), with your ideas.

Recent Titles

ASHE HIGHER EDUCATION REPORT
Order Form

SUBSCRIPTIONS AND SINGLE ISSUES

DISCOUNTED BACK ISSUES:

Use this form to receive **20% off** all back issues of ASHE Higher Education Report. All single issues priced at **$22.40** (normally $28.00)

TITLE	ISSUE NO.	ISBN
_____	_____	_____
_____	_____	_____
_____	_____	_____

Call 888-378-2537 or see mailing instructions below. When calling, mention the promotional code, JB7ND, to receive your discount.

SUBSCRIPTIONS: (1 year, 6 issues)

☐ New Order ☐ Renewal

U.S.	☐ Individual: $165	☐ Institutional: $199
Canada/Mexico	☐ Individual: $165	☐ Institutional: $235
All Others	☐ Individual: $201	☐ Institutional: $310

Call 888-378-2537 or see mailing and pricing instructions below. Online subscriptions are available at www.interscience.wiley.com.

Copy or detach page and send to:
John Wiley & Sons, Journals Dept, 5th Floor
989 Market Street, San Francisco, CA 94103-1741

Order Form can also be faxed to: 888-481-2665

Issue/Subscription Amount: $ _____
Shipping Amount: $ _____
(for single issues only—subscription prices include shipping)
Total Amount: $ _____

SHIPPING CHARGES:

SURFACE	Dometic	Canadian
First Item	$5.00	$6.00
Each Add'l Item	$3.00	$1.50

(No sales tax for U.S. subscriptions. Canadian residents, add GST for subscription orders. Individual rate subscriptions must be paid by personal check or credit card. Individual rate subscriptions may not be resold as library copies.)

☐ Payment enclosed (U.S. check or money order only. All payments must be in U.S. dollars.)

☐ VISA ☐ MC ☐ Amex # _____ Exp. Date _____

Card Holder Name _____ Card Issue # _____

Signature _____ Day Phone _____

☐ Bill Me (U.S. institutional orders only. Purchase order required.)

Purchase order # _____

Federal Tax ID13559302   GST 89102 8052

Name _____

Address _____

Phone _____ E-mail _____

ASHE-ERIC HIGHER EDUCATION REPORT
IS NOW AVAILABLE ONLINE AT WILEY INTERSCIENCE

What is Wiley InterScience?

Wiley InterScience is the dynamic online content service from John Wiley & Sons delivering the full text of over 300 leading scientific, technical, medical, and professional journals, plus major reference works, the acclaimed Current Protocols laboratory manuals, and even the full text of select Wiley print books online.

What are some special features of Wiley InterScience?

Wiley Interscience Alerts is a service that delivers table of contents via e-mail for any journal available on Wiley InterScience as soon as a new issue is published online.
Early View is Wiley's exclusive service presenting individual articles online as soon as they are ready, even before the release of the compiled print issue. These articles are complete, peer-reviewed, and citable.
CrossRef is the innovative multi-publisher reference linking system enabling readers to move seamlessly from a reference in a journal article to the cited publication, typically located on a different server and published by a different publisher.

How can I access Wiley InterScience?

Visit http://www.interscience.wiley.com.

Guest Users can browse Wiley InterScience for unrestricted access to journal Tables of Contents and Article Abstracts, or use the powerful search engine.
Registered Users are provided with a *Personal Home Page* to store and manage customized alerts, searches, and links to favorite journals and articles. Additionally, Registered Users can view free Online Sample Issues and preview selected material from major reference works.
Licensed Customers are entitled to access full-text journal articles in PDF, with select journals also offering full-text HTML.

How do I become an Authorized User?

Authorized Users are individuals authorized by a paying Customer to have access to the journals in Wiley InterScience. For example, a University that subscribes to Wiley journals is considered to be the Customer.
Faculty, staff and students authorized by the University to have access to those journals in Wiley InterScience are Authorized Users. Users should contact their Library for information on which Wiley journals they have access to in Wiley InterScience.

ASK YOUR INSTITUTION ABOUT WILEY INTERSCIENCE TODAY!